MARINE AQUARIA
— AND —
MINIATURE REEFS

THE FISHES, THE INVERTEBRATES, THE TECHNIQUES

t.f.h.

MARINE AQUARIA
— AND —
MINIATURE REEFS

THE FISHES, THE INVERTEBRATES, THE TECHNIQUES

From choosing and using the equipment right through picking the best tankmates and detecting and treating diseases—all by the world's foremost authority

DR. C.W. EMMENS

Distributed in the UNITED STATES by T.F.H. Publications, Inc., One T.F.H. Plaza, Neptune City, NJ 07753; in CANADA to the Pet Trade by H & L Pet Supplies Inc., 27 Kingston Crescent, Kitchener, Ontario N2B 2T6; Rolf C. Hagen Ltd., 3225 Sartelon Street, Montreal 382 Quebec; in CANADA to the Book Trade by Macmillan of Canada (A Division of Canada Publishing Corporation), 164 Commander Boulevard, Agincourt, Ontario M1S 3C7; in ENGLAND by T.F.H. Publications Limited, Cliveden House/Priors Way/Bray, Maidenhead, Berkshire SL6 2HP, England; in AUSTRALIA AND THE SOUTH PACIFIC by T.F.H. (Australia) Pty. Ltd., Box 149, Brookvale 2100 N.S.W., Australia; in NEW ZEALAND by Ross Haines & Son, Ltd., 82 D Elizabeth Knox Place, Panmure, Auckland, New Zealand; in the PHILIPPINES by Bio-Research, 5 Lippay Street, San Lorenzo Village, Makati Rizal; in SOUTH AFRICA by Multipet Pty. Ltd., Box 235, New Germany, South Africa 3620. Published by T.F.H. Publications, Inc. Manufactured in the United States of America by T.F.H. Publications, Inc.

CONTENTS

Marine aquaria can be fitted into almost any decor. Not only can a tank be custom made for a particular spot but many new fashion conscious designs are becoming available in pet shops. Photo courtesy of Mr. & Mrs. Werther Paccagnella.

The Tank
& Accessories

In this book, we shall suppose that you wish to set up a marine aquarium with a tank and equipment that are readily obtainable from a local aquarium store and that the job is to be done without undue expense. You can spend a great deal of money on ready-made, elaborate set-ups that won't do any more for you than a simple arrangement properly managed. You can spend equal amounts on equipment, special filters, sterilizers, ozonizers, protein skimmers, etc., that are only necessary in special circumstances and will not be needed at this stage of the game. Later, you may decide to own a "minireef" or similar aquarium that comes with all its works complete and enables the keeping of delicate organisms like living coral with good success, or to build your own version of it. But first, learn the basics while keeping to simple equipment.

A good, healthy growth of algae should be available when herbivores or omnivores like surgeonfishes and angelfishes are present. Photo by Kiyomi Eto.

THE TANK

Salt water attacks almost everything and it wasn't until the introduction of all-glass aquaria that amateur marine aquaria came into their own. Such aquaria are constructed only of glass and inert silicone rubber sealant and are unaffected by salt water. Plastic counterparts that do not scratch are now obtainable, but are more expensive and have no advantages except lightness and resistance to breakage or cracking.

The shape of a tank is dictated by *biology* and *elegance* working in opposition. *Biology* says a wide, shallow tank with as large a surface area as possible because this helps to aerate the water; *elegance* says a tall tank that looks much better and shows off its contents. So we usually compromise with dimensions of the order of, say, 36″ x 16″ x 20″ (length x width x height), although really large tanks will not be as relatively tall, say 72″ x 20″ x 26″.

Seawater aquaria are best as large as reasonable, for a number of reasons. A large volume of water is more stable in temperature, in constituents, and in alkalinity. It remains warm for a longer time, even if there is a power or heater failure. It holds a reasonable number of fishes or invertebrates, as marine aquaria cannot be as crowded as can freshwater ones.

Even in well managed marine aquaria brief skirmishes among the inhabitants may be unavoidable. These usually do not lead to any serious injury in an uncrowded tank. Photo by Kiyomi Eto.

However, it weighs a lot and costs more to purchase and to populate. So we compromise, and for a beginner we recommend something between 25 and 50 gallons. The 36″ x 16″ x 20″ aquarium is a nice size, and holds theoretically just under 50 gallons, but with gravel and rocks a figure nearer to 40 is more realistic. To calculate the gallon capacity,

multiply the three dimensions together and divide by 231.

A well-made tank is constructed from new plate glass. Do not accept scratched or second-hand material. Up to 12″ deep and 30″ long, thick window glass is sufficient (about ³⁄₁₆″) with a ¼″-plate base. From 12″ to 15″ deep, ¼″-plate should be used; above 15″, ³⁄₈″-plate; above 24″, ½″-plate. Any

Marine fishes should not be crowded. Although this tank can perhaps support a few more fishes it cannot support many more.

tank over 30″ long should have one or more 3″ to 6″ wide cross braces of glass from front to back, countersunk about ½″ below the top. Supports for cover glasses, also countersunk, should line the sides and be attached to the cross braces, so that, apart from small segments removed for cables and airlines, the top presents an even covered surface about ½″ below the edges of the glass. This prevents water and salt from running over the outside.

An aquarium of the size recommended will give no trouble if placed on a regular stand, table,or piece of

Two successful but different aquarium set-ups. The upper tank has more coral decorations; the lower tank has much more algae and plant life. Both are doing well. Photos by Kiyomi Eto.

furniture. Heavier tanks may well do so, as water weighs 8¼ lbs per gallon. It must be evenly supported on a dead level surface - best done by first checking with a level, then placing a layer of ¼″ or ½″ styrofoam where the tank is to go. This will take up any small irregularities in tank or support. Place the best face to the front, get help, and lower the tank carefully into position. It may help, where feasible, to tape the styrofoam temporarily in position so that it doesn't slip about while the tank is being lowered.

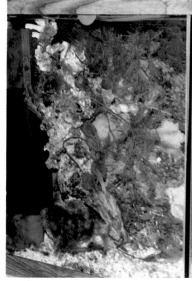

▲ In this tank the non-fish element is dominant. Invertebrates and algae (*Caulerpa*) are apparently thriving under a good diet and proper lighting conditions respectively. Photo by Dr. Herbert R. Axelrod.

LIGHTING

It is best not to place an aquarium where it gets too much daylight, as this is uncontrolled and can overheat the tank if it receives direct sunlight. Instead, a reflecting hood and top light is provided, almost always fluorescent. It doesn't heat the water and is cheap to run, although not to install. Modern fluorescent tubes are also available in many spectral types from which to choose. If you are only going to keep fishes, any tube will do, so just suit yourself. Some enhance the fishes' colors, others copy natural daylight or give a warmer light if preferred, but all will give enough light from just one tube running the length of the aquarium. If you wish to cultivate seaweeds (higher algae) or to keep some invertebrates such as anemones, stronger light is needed and, in a 36″ tank, at least 2 tubes should be used. Just how many depends on the light they provide, as types of

These two tanks are also well managed and contain healthy fishes. Note the judicious use of artificial plants in both tanks. Live plants are currently being successfully kept more and more in marine tanks. Photos by Kiyomi Eto. ▼

tube differ very considerably in output. Consult your supplier and, if you are lucky, he'll know.

The light should be switched on for at least 12 hours per day, longer doesn't matter, although you may find that some fishes put themselves to bed early. However, don't switch the lights ON or OFF in an otherwise dark room as it tends to panic fishes. See that the room light, or daylight, is ON first and last. Keep as far as you can to a regular schedule to which the fishes can become accustomed.

Two mini-reef tanks. The lower one has a very large surface area with five separate light fixtures. The bulbs can be selected depending upon the needs of the animals and plants housed in the tank. Photo by Dr. Herbert R. Axelrod.

HEATING

Unless in a constantly warm room, a tropical tank needs a thermostat/heater combination, usually together in one instrument. Choose one in which the temperature can be altered from the outside, whether it is totally submersible or not, and guaranteed to be suitable for salt water. On the whole, a totally submersible heater laid at the bottom of the tank is best as it is unobtrusive, efficient, and not in danger of shattering because you forgot to switch it off when making a water change.

Do not buy too powerful a heater since if it sticks in the ON position it will cook the tank contents. One that can raise the temperature about 20°F above room temperature is normally adequate, for a 20- to 30-gallon tank 100 watts is enough; for a 40- to 50-gallon tank, 150 watts; 60-80 gallons, 200 watts.

A thermometer is also needed. Get either an alcohol-containing (usually red) one or a stick-on type for the outside of the tank. Mercury thermometers poison the water if accidentally broken. The stick-on, liquid crystal thermometer will tend to read a little low, just a degree or so, but that doesn't matter. Check your thermometer by some means; your druggist will usually do it against an accurate one to make sure it isn't badly out—they can be.

AERATION

Practically all marine aquaria need some form of aeration, although this may be combined with filtration. The purpose of aeration is to stir the water, particularly at its surface, so that the water in the aquarium is

Devices that signal a warning when the temperature in a tank exceeds prescribed limits are available.

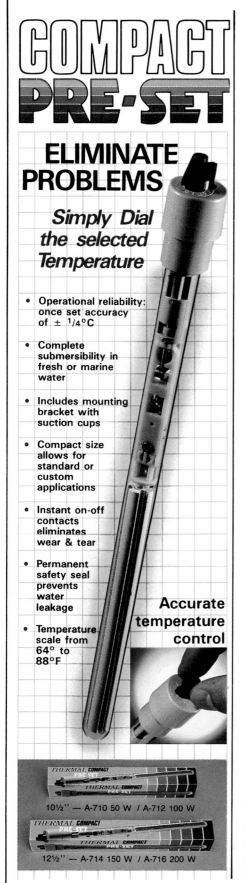

constantly brought up into contact with the air above it, with which it exchanges gases. Oxygen is absorbed and carbon dioxide is released into the air, while the water movement created is beneficial to the fishes, accustomed to it in the wild.

You will notice that large bubbles just "glug" up to the surface without doing much stirring, while very small ones form a fine mist and also have little effect. The best bubble size is 1/30th to 1/50th of an inch in diameter, which carries most water with it. There is some gas exchange between the bubbles themselves and the water, but it is small in comparison with the surface exchange. Marine fishes need a high oxygen content in the water, hence the need for as efficient an arrangement as we can devise. The best airstones to use are of fused ceramic or similar material; wooden ones give very fine bubbles and clog up easily.

An air pump will be needed to operate the airstones and filter, although the latter may have a water pump instead. A good brand of diaphragm pump will be adequate, but make sure that it is quiet in operation (often difficult to do in a retail store). You will also need air-lines and gang valves to run from the pump to the equipment. Buy soft, manageable tubing that goes where you want it to, and not where it wants, and take home a yard or two more than you think you'll need.

Heaters are important components of any aquarium. The lives of your animals depend upon the accuracy and dependability of the thermostats and heating elements.

REGULAR MODEL

SUPER MODEL

Several types of oxygenators (to increase the supply of oxygen to the tank) are available in a well-stocked pet shop. These two are manufactured by Meridian Industries Aquarium Products.

FILTRATION

This is another "must". Filters do several things beside merely removing obvious dirt from the water. If fine enough, they can even take out algae and bacteria. These actions are called "mechanical." In addition, a filter can have a "chemical" action if its contents include a substance like activated carbon or coral sand. Carbon can remove unwanted chemicals; coral can help regulate the pH. Finally, a filter can develop a biological action if left undisturbed for long enough for bacteria to grow in it that help to convert wastes, especially ammonia, to harmless compounds.

Filters come in so many forms that it would take a book to describe them all, but we shall be concerned with only two types, a simple carbon filter and an undergravel biological filter, working together. Finely divided activated carbon, or charcoal, comes in a pinhead size and consists of dull looking granules that have an incredibly large total surface area, as they are pitted and channelled throughout. This is not the filter "coals" often sold, which are useless. High grade activated carbon can take up over 50% of its own weight of impurities from the water, including coloring matter, toxins and toxic gases, heavy metals, sugars and many other organic compounds, and antibiotics and various other

medications. It also takes up vitamins and trace elements, so is not without disadvantages. Only a few ounces are needed in a 30- to 50-gallon aquarium, well washed before use (preferably in salt water), to remove dust. This will last for several months before needing renewal.

An undergravel filter uses the gravel at the bottom of the aquarium as the filter bed and allows the growth of vast numbers of beneficial bacteria that primarily convert ammonia, the end product of the decay of excreta and uneaten food or dead animals, to first nitrites and then nitrates. Ammonia and nitrites are poisonous. Nitrates are almost harmless and can be allowed to accumulate to a

A selection of White Shark products useful in filtering a marine tank.

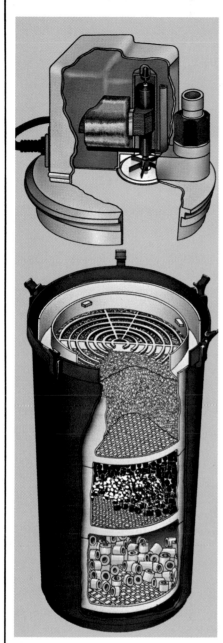

considerable extent. Ammonia is the worst toxin, lethal in less than one part per million (1 ppm or 1 mg/liter), and becoming more lethal with higher pH (the measure of acidity or alkalinity of the water; pH 7 is neutral, pH 6 slightly acid and pH 8 slightly alkaline). As sea water is approximately pH 8.3, ammonia is about ten times as poisonous in it as in neutral water. A carbon filter doesn't take up much of the ammonia, nitrites, or nitrates, the products of the nitrogen cycle, and so the two filters complement one another.

THE CARBON FILTER

A simple "box" filter is sufficient for carbon filtration and may be located either inside or outside the aquarium. The best type is probably an inside corner filter. It fits neatly in one corner at the bottom rear of the aquarium. A central stem carries a rising stream of bubbles that causes water to flow through a perforated lid, down through the filter bed and up through the central stem back into the tank. The few ounces of carbon are sandwiched between layers of filter pad to keep them in place and to remove gross particles. The top pad may need replacing every week or two as it clogs up, but the rest can be left for much longer. Hidden by rock or coral, this filter is quite unobtrusive.

If you wish, a filter can instead be hung either inside or outside the tank at the top and be more accessible, although more visible too. An inside filter can be a simple box with a perforated base, carrying the

An exploded view of a typical canister filter. The types of filter media may be changed depending upon need and usage.

◄

Any of the various types of filtering material shown at the left of this canister can be used depending upon the job the filter is expected to do. One of them is shown in place in the filter.

A simple corner box filter can be an efficient device and useful in carbon filtration.

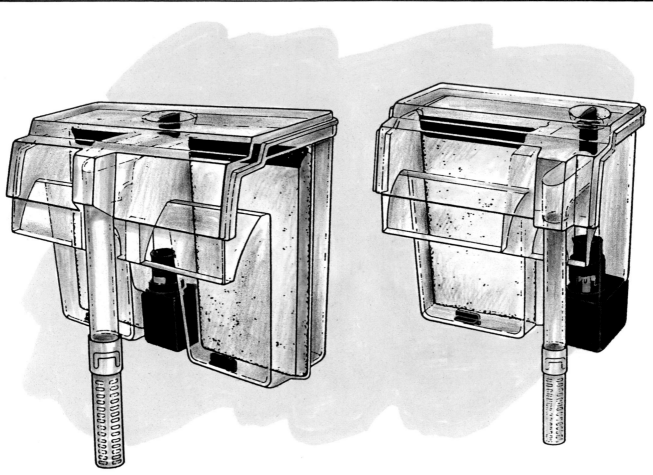

Outside power filters are commonly the filter type chosen by aquarists. They are efficient and easy to clean. These filters come in various sizes corresponding to the standard tank sizes available. Two filters are often used on one tank for greater filtering capacity and to enable the aquarist to clean one filter while the other remains operating.

Different methods of providing an air lift for undergravel filters. As you can see not all methods are equally efficient.

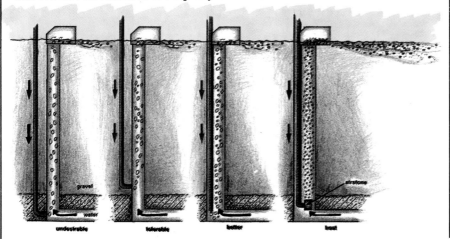

carbon "sandwich" as before. An airlift then conveys water to the box whence it flows down through the filter and back into the tank. An airlift is a long tube carrying water from near the base of the tank by a similar rising stream of bubbles to that of the corner filter. An outside filter is a little more complicated. The airlift carries water from the filter back to the tank, while siphons bring it from the tank into the filter. Since the filter is outside the tank it must not be able to overflow, and this arrangement insures that it can't.

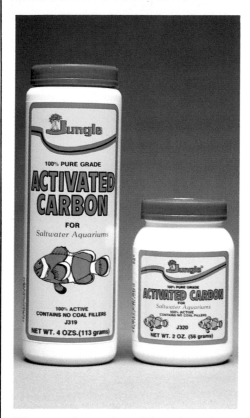

Filter media, such as this activated carbon, are now specially packaged for the saltwater aquarium.

The basic principle of filtration is simply to pump the water into a filter box, canister, or whatever, so that it is forced to flow through a filter medium. The filter medium removes much of the larger suspended material from the water before the water is returned to the aquarium.

Some filters are quite complicated pieces of technology. This Hockney Aquaria Filtration System is a combination filter/heater/protein skimmer all in one.

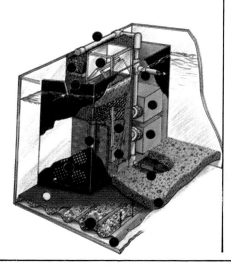

THE UNDERGRAVEL FILTER

The best type of undergravel filter is a perforated or slotted plastic plate or plates raised about ½″ above the glass bottom of the tank and covering the entire base. At one or more places at the rear of the tank, airlifts raise water from under the plate to the surface, or water pumps (power heads) do the same job more efficiently. Over the plate is placed coral sand or any other suitable calcium-containing mineral in a finely divided state. It should be at an average depth of about 3″, nowhere less than 2″, and of a particle size ⅒″ to ⅕″, *i.e.* too big to pass through the slots in the filter plate.

The usual commercial article offered today has an airstone assisted airlift, the tube being wide enough to allow a small airstone to fit at the base and deliver its bubbles eventually across the surface of the water, thus giving good aeration as well. A power head similarly pumps the water across the surface, or just under it in some models, in which case additional aeration will be needed unless built into the power head itself. Either arrangement must give a flow of around 3 times the tank volume per hour to be maximally efficient. To ensure that no substrate gets under the filter and so may clog it up, it is best

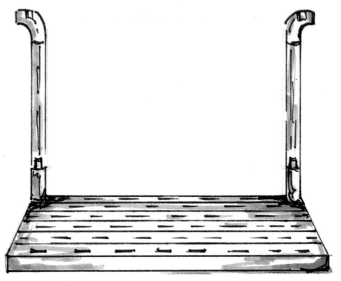

For smaller tanks undergravel filters may be a single piece that covers the entire bottom. In larger tanks it is sometimes necessary to use several undergravel filters working together. Illustration by Lisa Marie O'Connell.

Some tanks are manufactured with built-in filtration systems. This complete unit is very efficient.

to cover the whole plate with plastic flyscreen before adding the gravel.

This undergravel filter is *never* to be completely disturbed unless for a very good reason. Once it is in full action it is a living, breathing entity essential to the well-being of the aquarium. If more than a fraction of it is siphoned off it loses potency and the fishes will suffer. At most, a quarter of it can safely be removed in cleaning, and not all from the top layers that are the most active part of the filter. Methods for starting it up are discussed later.

OTHER EQUIPMENT

That about covers the basic requirements of the tank itself, except for rockwork, coral, or other decorations. We shall need a few auxiliary tools, however. These are:

A *hydrometer* to measure the salinity (salt content) of the water. It is a bulbous instrument with a long graduated stem that floats at a depth dependent on the amount of dissolved salts, and thus measures the specific gravity of the water. This is 1.025 at 60°F in average sea water, or about 1.022 at 80°F on a hydrometer designed, as most are, to measure at 60°F. However, some are specifically made for aquaria and may be set for 75°F or 80°F. Inquire when buying one. As an alternative, an instrument is now available with a pointer readout.

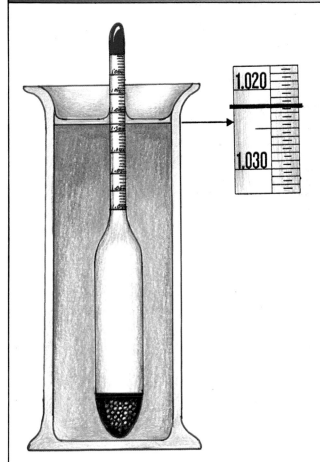

A simple hydrometer is used to measure the specific gravity of the seawater. This should be 1.022 at 80°F on a hydrometer designed to measure at 60°F.

A net or nets for handling fishes, about ½ the tank width square, with a pocket 6"-12" deep.

A *siphon* for cleaning the tank. This is best made of a 1/2" glass or rigid plastic tube about the same depth as the tank. At one end, attach several feet of tubing, so that a bucket on the floor is easily reached and at the other end just a few inches of the same to prevent glass-against-rockwork collisions. Rubber tubing is much easier to handle than plastic tubing when controlling waterflow. *A dip tube,* just a glass tube this time a little longer than the tank depth so that you can take up uneaten food, etc., when necessary.

A pair of *plastic tongs* to reach awkward corners are very useful too.

Kits to measure pH and nitrite concentrations, to be used as explained later on.

Sodium bicarbonate to adjust the pH and retain the buffering capacity of the water, to be used on a regular basis as explained later on.

A high-grade salt mix for when you start operations or change water.

Certain siphoning/refilling devices used for filling freshwater tanks can be used to remove water from large marine aquaria.

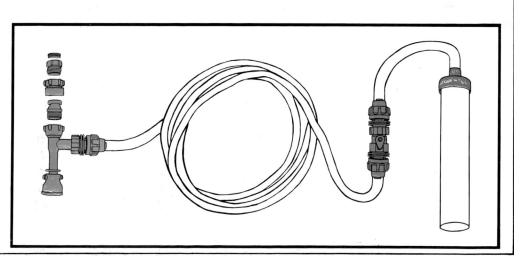

This is an example of an internal canister power filter. Some aquarists prefer the internal filter because it can be hidden behind the tank decorations; others begrudge the space it takes up in the tank.

Extra Gadgetry

There are a number of sometimes quite expensive pieces of equipment that have grown up around aquarium keeping, particularly of marine aquaria. Most are designed to remove even more effectively the waste products produced or to sterilize the water as far as possible. None is necessary with a well-kept tank, but you may be urged to purchase one or another, or indeed several, and the best advice is DON'T. This is not to assert that they are useless, far from it, merely superfluous at your present stage of marine aquarium keeping.

Powered canister filters force the water through fine filter blocks that remove even bacteria and really clean the water. Expensive and liable to give trouble.

Eheim, one of the popular brands of canister filter, provides a filter designed for almost any size aquarium. Some aquarists use these canister filters in tandem when setting up a minireef aquarium.

Protein skimmers (air-strippers, foam fractionators) pass a stream of bubbles up a column of tank water with an arrangement to collect the foam that forms if the water is polluted. This foam contains many types of contaminants. However, carbon does the same thing.

Ozone (O_3) is a super-active form of oxygen produced by special ozonizing equipment. It kills bacteria and parasites and oxidizes some toxins. It is hazardous to introduce directly into the aquarium, so special arrangements have to be made to use it. It may, for instance be used in a protein skimmer.

Ultraviolet light (UV) is another sterilizer, also to be applied outside the aquarium as it is harmful to life if it is exposed directly to it. Both UV and ozone are more applicable to the laboratory than in the home.

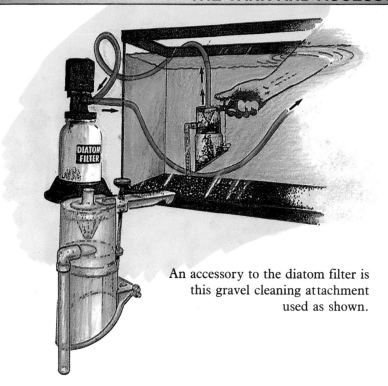

An accessory to the diatom filter is this gravel cleaning attachment used as shown.

Many types of canister filters have been developed. This one is courtesy of Project SRL, Italy.

Diatom filters are normally used for limited time periods on a regular basis rather than for constant filtration.

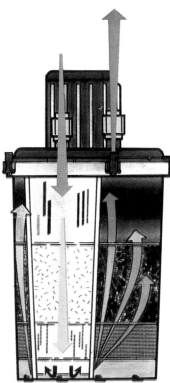

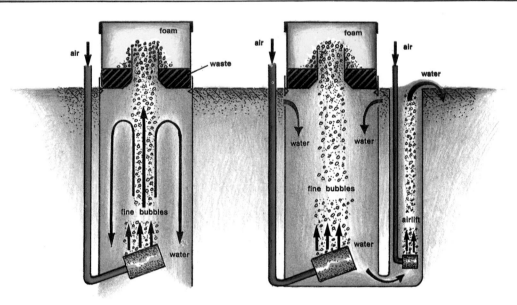

Protein skimmers work by using a rising stream of bubbles to carry many types of contaminants into a collecting chamber via a foam. Protein skimmers are also called air-strippers or foam fractionators.

Many aquarists use combinations of filtering methods. Here, for example, an undergravel filter is combined with a canister filter. Each aquarist must decide which filtering system he is comfortable with.

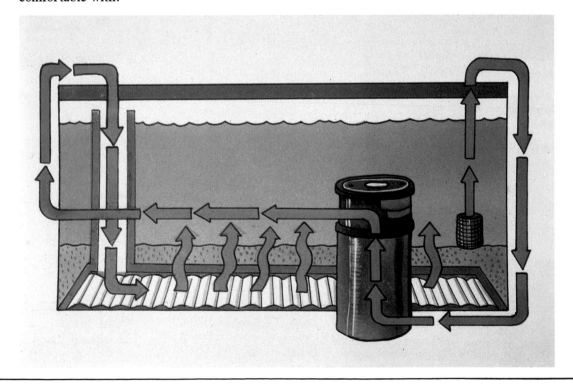

Setting up the Aquarium

There is an order for setting up an aquarium that makes the task easy and future management as simple as possible. We shall suppose that all material has been purchased and that an undergravel filter with an auxiliary carbon filter is to be used as recommended.

1. Wash all materials thoroughly, especially the coral sand or whatever is to be used. It may need ten or twenty successive washings, ¼-bucket at a time, in tap water, with thorough stirring. This will be the worst task you face and may take a couple of hours, but it is well worth the trouble as failure to get the substrate really clean at the start can result in cloudy water that is difficult to get clear. You will be surprised at how much muck can come out of even "washed" sand or gravel.

2. So arrange the undergravel filter so it fits snugly against the back and sides of the aquarium. Leave a small margin of ½" or so at the front so that it is not visible after the gravel has been added. Connect any airlifts or other tubing that serves the filter. Cover the filter with a double thickness of plastic flyscreen and tuck it down on all sides, with particular care that no access except through the flyscreen is left to the underside of the filter. Cut the flyscreen to fit around uplifts, etc.

3. Using wet gravel, which is more handleable than if dry, cover the filter to a depth of several inches, sloping it gently

The mini-reef system normally contains a preponderance of invertebrates and only a few fishes such as seen here. The equipment necessary for the maintenance of this aquarium is kept in the cabinet below the tank.

from back and sides to middle front so as to form a shallow half-basin not less than 2″ – 3″ deep anywhere. This looks nice and helps to steer the mulm to the front where it is easily removed. It also assists the filter to act in a uniform manner as the shallower layer of gravel at front is furthest from the uplifts. Seed the gravel with the desirable bacteria that will convert ammonia to nitrates.

This can be done with a few pinches of garden soil, a commercial preparation from your dealer, or more riskily because of disease fears, some gravel from an established tank believed to be disease-free. The commercial preparation available at your petshop is to be preferred if available.

4. Place rocks, coral, etc., in position. Make sure that they are thoroughly cured, coral in

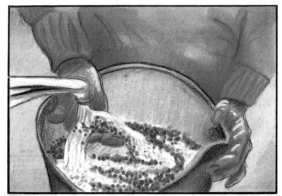

Wash all materials thoroughly.

Add measured amount of sea salt.

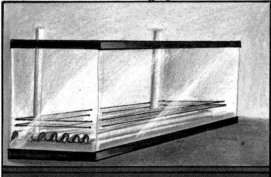

Place undergravel filter in tank.

Fill tank up to proper level.

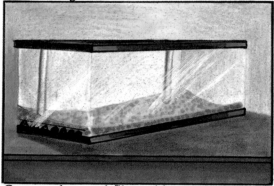

Cover undergravel filter with gravel.

Turn everything on.

Place rocks, coral, etc. in position.

After conditioning tank, add animals.

particular. If in any doubt, sit coral in a bucket of *fresh water* for a few days. If it is not clean you will see it or smell it! Only use rocks that have been guaranteed safe in salt water. Sandstone free of iron, granite, marble, and old compacted dead coral are good rocks. At the same time place the heater, airstone(s), and corner filter (if used) in position and hidden as far as possible. If necessary, fix airlines and leads in position with rocks or coral so that they do not float up consequently. Place the heater away from contact with the glass and see that it cannot move onto it later, but do not cover or bury it in any way. Do not trust suckers to keep a heater in position.

5. Make a guess at the actual volume of water the tank will now hold, allowing for everything placed inside it— 20% off the calculated gallon capacity is a good guide. Then dump in your artificial salts, using a good grade that preferably divulges its formula,

For the marine aquarist who wants to start with a sterile water environment there are salt mixes available. The water can be mixed in a separate container and added to the tank as needed.

Chemicals are available to remove chlorine, chloramine, and ammonia from your water helping to reduce the waiting time when setting up your tank.

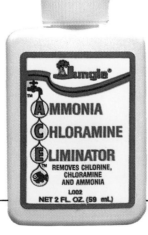

at 4 oz per gallon. Fine adjustments can be made later on. There is no need to dissolve the salts before filling the aquarium, although you will have to do it subsequently. Unless your tap water is known to be safe, guard against the possible presence of chloramines (substances added to destroy bacteria, etc.) by adding 1 grain per gallon of sodium thiosulphate (photographers' "hypo") or a commercial water purifier. If only chlorine is known to be present, forget it as it will disappear when the equipment starts up.

6. Place a bowl in center front and lead your hose into it, after having run the water for some minutes to clear the pipes of any stagnant water that may be contaminated. Gently turn on the hose so that water runs slowly over the top of the bowl with least possible disturbance to the gravel. Half fill the tank and then stop and wait for a few hours to let some of the salt dissolve and also to check for leaks. (Not very likely, but it's best to be sure.) Then complete the filling, by which time much of the salt will have formed a thick brine at the bottom, but some constituents such as the

calcium salts may still be undissolved. If you happen to be able to use natural sea water, pour it into a bowl gently with a plastic watering can.

7. Now for the first test! Turn everything on. See that the airstones and filters are operating well, not too briskly, just a nice steady flow. Watch the temperature rise and see that it levels out at between 76° and 80°F. When all is well, test the specific gravity with the hydrometer. It should read between 1.022 and 1.023 to copy natural sea-water, but if fishes alone are to be accommodated it is quite in order to have it a little lower, not less than 1.018 or you will have trouble introducing the fishes. Let the tank run for a day or two and if all continues to be well, go ahead.

MATURATION OF THE TANK

The aquarium is now ready for a conditioning process that will in general be unfamiliar to freshwater aquarists and that arises primarily because of the higher pH of the marine environment. As already noted,

This water conditioner is used when starting a new tank. It is faster and cleaner than the old fashioned method.

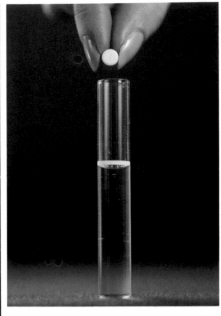

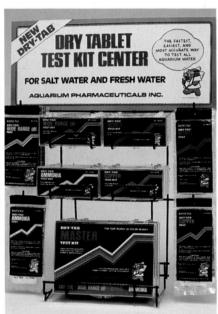

Keeping tabs on the water quality of your tank is very important. There are kits that are designed for testing the water every step of the way.

this means that the toxicity of ammonia is much increased in comparison with the average freshwater aquarium. If many fishes or any other creatures are put into a newly set-up marine tank, a condition known as *the new tank syndrome* will almost surely result. After a week or so, the fishes begin to look miserable, with clamped fins, rapid respiration, and quite probably an outbreak of disease. Untreated, many or all will soon die.

Why does this happen? It is because the fishes are producing ammonia that accumulates in the water and poisons them. The bacteria that would break it down are not present in sufficient numbers. Only frequent and considerable water changes over several weeks will save them, if it is not already too late. It so happens that the bacteria concerned (*Nitrosomonas* species convert ammonia to nitrites and

Bacteria and enzymes needed for conditioning your tank can be purchased at your nearest pet shop.

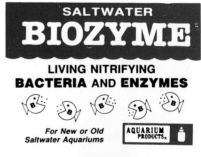

Nitrobacter species carry this on to nitrates) are very slow growing compared with normal ones. No method of breaking in a new tank can hurry things up very much. The process takes three to four weeks whatever you do, short of transferring a great deal of old mature gravel from another tank.

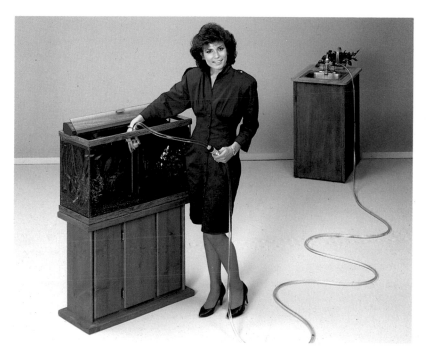

So what to do? Until recently, knowledgeable aquarists took the slow but sure route of adding fishes or invertebrates very gradually, so that the fish population growth accompanied bacterial growth. By that method the process could take several months. As an alternative, they put turtles or even some decaying meat or fish in the tank and accomplished the job that way. Then it occurred to someone to add ammonia directly to the aquarium. If it worked as it should, and the right amount was given, the process could be made as rapid as feasible and there would be theoretical

advantages that seem to work out in practice. First, most of the fishes could be put in together once the tank is mature, avoiding fighting and a prolonged wait. Second, if high but safe amounts of ammonia were added from the start, most of the bacteria developed in the filter would be desirable ones

Aquarium chores are becoming easier thanks to new products that can be used in either marine or freshwater tanks. The model here is demonstrating the use of a gravel cleaner.

instead of the usual mixed population that is found; so more fishes could eventually be housed.

CHEMICAL MATURATION

Methods for calculating how much ammonia to add day by day are complicated and depend on the water flow, gravel size, depth and other factors. As a general rule, if the recommendations above have been followed, an aquarium should receive the following schedule of doses:

Make up a 10% solution of ammonium chloride or a 15% solution of ammonium sulphate. These contain about the same amounts of ammonia (NH_3). You will need 250 ml of either solution per 25 gallons of sea water to complete the treatment (approximately ½ pint). Starting the treatment, add 2 ml (just under 1/2 standard 5 ml teaspoon) per 25 gallons on days 1 and 2; 4 ml (just under 1 teaspoon) on days 3 and 4; 6 ml (just over 1 teaspoon) on days 5 and 6; 8 ml (1-1/2 teaspoons) on days 7 and 8; from day 9 onwards add 10 ml (2 teaspoons) per day. While this is going on, purchase a nitrite kit and start to measure the nitrite level every other day from day 18 onwards, when a peak of nitrite production is to be expected. This peak will rise from next to nothing to 10 or 20 parts per million (ppm) and then fall again. When the level has fallen nearly to nil (less than 1 ppm) stop the ammonia treatment and put in the fishes within a day or two, nearly all at once.

When you compare these recommendations with others you may wonder at the amounts

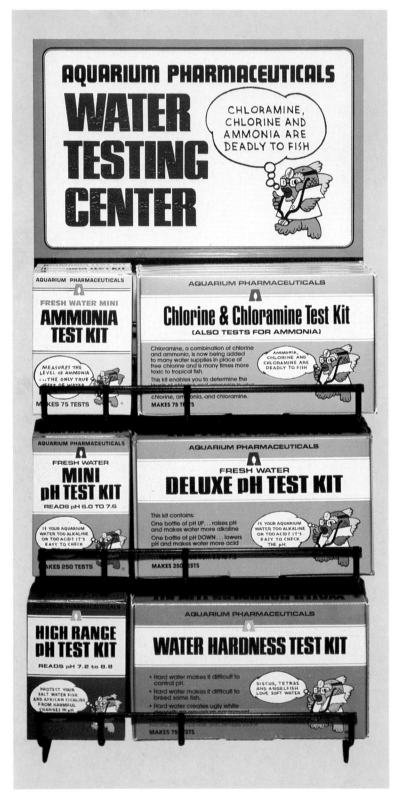

A variety of test kits are available for both freshwater and marine aquaria. Make sure you obtain the proper kit for use in a marine tank as the ranges differ. For example, the marine test kit for pH must include the high range (pH 7.2-9.0), whereas the fresh water kit should read lower (pH 6.0-7.6).

of ammonia salts used, but they are such as would on average be excreted per day by a full load of fishes—the equivalent of about 2.5 ppm ammonia per day, that the undergravel filter is demonstrably handling via the nitrogen cycle. Any smaller amounts would require the gradual introduction of fishes just as before. Note that a nitrite peak will occur with smaller amounts, but it won't indicate full capacity of the filter.

FISH CAPACITY OF TANKS

The numbers of fishes of different sizes that can be safely housed in a marine aquarium set-up as described cannot be as specifically stated as for a freshwater tropical tank. They depend on species and on feeding rates to a much greater extent than for freshwater fishes, and less on surface area because of the brisk circulation. However, if we follow usual maintenance procedures and don't over-feed, some rules can be suggested.

The feeding rate has a big effect; an unfed fish produces less than half the pollutants that a fish receiving 2.5% of its own body weight per day produces, and less than a third of those produced if 5% is fed per day (this refers to the wet weight of food, not flakes or other dry foods, for which the wet weight can be divided by 5 or 10).

A safe rule is to start a conditioned tank with a load of not more than one 1″ to 2″ fish per 5 gallons, allowing for growth to 2″ to 4″. As the tank, and the aquarist, matures even further, a suggested upper limit is a 2″ to 4″ fish per 3 gallons, but not all to be as big as 4″.

A designer tank can be a truly beautiful addition to any room. Notice how the decorations (including a live anemone) are gradually larger toward the wall end of the tank. The decorations are also placed in the center of the tank for better viewing. Photo compliments of Aqua Module.

It is best to have all elements of your set-up in hand before you start. This way there are no interruptions to head for the pet shop when you find you have forgotten something.

This is supposing near to expert care and maintenance and reasonably tough fishes like anemonefishes or wrasses. It would be dangerous with chaetodons and many others. So at the start, don't put more than 5 fishes in a 25-gallon tank or 10 in a 50-gallon one, and avoid the more delicate species. Don't overfeed but follow the rule of giving a bit less than they would eat practically straight away, twice a day at most. As the weeks pass, note the growth of the fishes. If they are visibly growing, all is well. If they are really shooting ahead, cut the food down a bit. Fishes are very accommodating and do not suffer if kept on a low diet as long as it is nourishing; moreover they are very thrifty convertors of food into flesh or energy.

PERIODIC MAINTENANCE

Regular servicing of the aquarium is necessary to keep it healthy. The exact timing of some of the items below can be varied according to circumstances; some may need to be more frequent and others less frequent than suggested, but all must be attended to at regular intervals.

Daily: Give the tank a general once-over. Check the temperature, airlifts, and appearance of the inhabitants. This can be done at feeding time, when any fish not eating should be noted for further observations.

Weekly: Clean glass covers and, if necessary, remove algae from the inside front glass. You may choose to leave a growth of algae on the back and sides.

Soft encrusting algae come away with ease if rubbed with a sponge or cloth ball on a stick, but limey types may need a razor blade scraper. Immersion of a clean blade in sea-water is harmless as long as you don't take too long.

Add one teaspoon per 25 gallons of sodium bicarbonate to preserve the pH and buffer capacity of the water.

Monthly: Siphon off 20 to 25% of the water, taking the opportunity to lift rocks gently to remove debris. Stir up the gravel surface for the same reason. The rubber tip to your siphon makes this a simple and safe procedure without having to plunge your arm into the tank. Check the state of the carbon filter (this may well be needed more often) and renew the top pad if necessary. Check the pH, nitrite level and specific

Products for the marine aquarium hobby have proliferated in recent years. These blocks help replace trace elements that are used up.

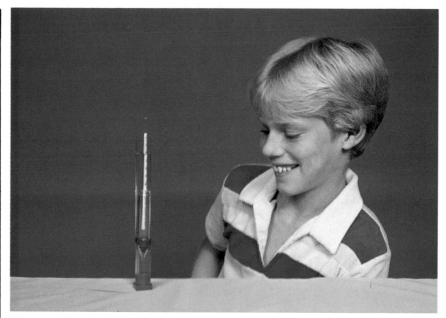

The specific gravity of your sea water can easily be checked by use of a simple hydrometer. This should be done routinely at least once a month, or whenever water is added or removed.

gravity. *Use fresh water to make up evaporation, not salt.*
Quarterly: Renew the carbon in the filter, washing the new carbon first. If the coral is covered by too much algae, remove some of it. Scrub the algae off, perhaps replacing some by spare heads of coral. Bleach those removed in the sun. A mix of various degrees of algal covering looks natural and attractive. This procedure may well have to be carried out more frequently. If necessary, coral can be bleached with household chlorine bleach, but rinse it very thoroughly before replacing it.

Yearly: Siphon off not more than ⅓rd of the gravel if a lot of muck swirls up as you disturb it. Rinse it thoroughly but not harshly and return it to the tank. This measure is needed if the airlifts are gurgling, indicating blockage of the undergravel filter. The task is best performed in several stages at weekly

intervals, removing ⅓rd of the surface and about ¹⁄₁₀th of the gravel at each. The top layers contribute most to the biological actions of the filter. After such a clean-up, feed lightly for the next week or so. Check over all mechanical equipment, pumps, valves, and their connections.

A number of artificial salt water mixes are available. Most are excellent. Be sure to follow directions carefully.

The larger marine tanks can house some of the adult fishes that are so appealing to aquarists. Marine tanks of 100-gallon capacity or larger are not unusual in the hobby. Photo by Dr. Herbert R. Axelrod.

Purchasing and Handling Fishes

A newly set up aquarium is by no means sterile, as we have seen, but it shouldn't have much in the way of dangerous organisms in it. If artificial salts have been used, no disease organisms should be present except those that float in from the air. Few of these will be capable of causing trouble, even fewer in a marine aquarium than in a freshwater one. One thing, therefore, that we want to do is to keep things that way. We shall not entirely succeed, but we may as well do our best and ward off trouble as much as possible. This means buying fishes from as disease-free a source as we can and even then not taking unnecessary risks. The best solution is to quarantine all newly-purchased fishes. During the quarantine period treat for the more likely diseases just in case. If you feel that you can trust your dealer to have done this for you, and very few do, you can take the risk; otherwise quarantine is strongly advisable.

If you are going to keep only fishes, it is possible to use the new tank itself as a quarantine tank, as by the chemical method of maturing it, the main batch of fishes can be introduced together and a suitable treatment given. If only a very few subsequent small introductions will be made, repeat treatments may be in order, too. If keeping invertebrates is contemplated, even at some later stage, it is not advisable to introduce any treatments to the aquarium unless absolutely necessary. This is because many invertebrates are killed by such measures. In that case, a separate small quarantine tank set up as was the main aquarium should be contemplated, or you are taking risks. A 10- or 15-gallon tank is adequate.

BUYING FISHES

Before buying anything live from a pet shop, look carefully around the place and even more carefully at any tank from which you may purchase a fish. If anything seems wrong with any of the tanks, be warned. If anything seems wrong with any fish in a particular tank, buy nothing from it. Slightly torn fins or tail, not inflamed or sore looking, can be ignored, but nothing worse.

Purchasing fishes for your tank is an important step. Buying from a reputable dealer will help ensure that you will start with healthy fishes and that a quarantine period may not be necessary. Photo by Dr. Herbert R. Axelrod.

Look not only for signs of disease such as visible spots or sores, clamped fins, or glancing off coral or rocks, but at the general condition of fishes. They should be plump, alert, and should take food. Ask the dealer to offer some. A hollow belly or "razor back" with wasted back muscles are bad signs indicating that the fish has been starving. A particularly bad condition, not easy to spot, is encountered in the cyanide-poisoned fish. Those fishes that survive capture when cyanide is pumped into the water are often sufficiently poisoned that they cannot digest food. As a result, they may have full tummies and look O.K. at first, but they are going to perish in a few weeks from starvation. The only real guarantee is the dealer who can assure you that his fishes have

not been caught with cyanide. Regrettably, not too many can. Other things to look for before purchase are normal respiration, or gilling, and general behavior. The gills of an undisturbed small fish should not show more than 100 movements per minute, fewer in large specimens. Parasites often infect the gills first and impede respiration. The fins should be neither clamped nor kept erect and should be in constant motion as the fish moves around alertly in the water. A few reef fishes, such as gobies and wrasses, hide away normally, but the great majority should not do so. Look also for clear, healthy eyes and no signs of damage around the mouth, a frequent source of trouble.

Carefully observe the fishes that you expect to purchase for any signs of disease or aberrant behavior. Make sure you watch them at feeding time to see if they are actively feeding and what type of foods they prefer. Photo by Dr. Herbert R. Axelrod.

TAKING FISHES HOME

Guard against temperature changes when transporting all fishes. They will be in relatively small volumes of water in plastic bags and liable to rapid upward or downward shifts in temperature unless carried in an insulated container. So go to collect them armed with a big enough styrofoam box or other suitable means of transport.

They must now be transferred either to quarantine or the main tank. Float the plastic bag in the tank after checking the pH and the temperature, if necessary of both. If there is more than a few tenths of a pH difference or a few degrees, say 3°F, in temperature, take one to two hours over the following, if not, ½ hour will do. Gradually replace the water in the bag with that from the tank; a 25% change per time is about right, at 10 - 30 minute intervals, according to the differences. Then allow the fish to swim gently into the tank. Salinity changes are unlikely to be a problem unless you keep your tank particularly dilute.

Keep an eye on the newly-introduced fishes for an hour or so, to see that all appears well. If others are already in the aquarium look for aggression, as marine fishes are often very pugnacious, especially toward newcomers. Don't panic at a little bickering and chasing as long as it dies down. If it doesn't, switch off the lights to see if that stops it. If not, you may have to remove either a particular bully or his victim and try again later. Shift the scenery around a fair bit, a trick that often confuses the old inhabitants and stops their aggressiveness.

The plastic bags containing the new fishes should be floated in the tank after checking the pH and temperature. The water in the bag should then be gradually exchanged for tank water over a period of up to 30 minutes. Illustration by John R. Quinn.

QUARANTINE

Whether to quarantine is up to you. If you are reasonably sure of your supplier you may decide to risk avoiding the trouble of doing so. *But it is a risk.* Most times you will probably get away with it, then on the next occasion you'll regret it! We all do it, sometimes unavoidably, and sooner or later we are sorry. Fishes in an established aquarium often have a degree of immunity to some of the commoner diseases and so the aquarist may get careless, having taken risks in the past successfully, or apparently so. Then in comes a new fish with the "galloping Egyptian pox" or whatnot, and there's trouble, or a healthy new fish catches a disease from the tank.

Quarantine procedures vary. Some aquarists quarantine the fishes for, say, 3 weeks, a reasonable period. If nothing happens they transfer them to the aquarium. Others routinely treat with one "cure" or another, usually copper or copper plus formalin, and then transfer. Some even dunk all new fishes in fresh water for a minute or two and then treat for disease in the quarantine tank in addition. The fresh water dunk is a bit hazardous and should be confined to tough fishes, with careful watch over how they react, but it does burst open surface parasites including velvet and much of white spot, because of the osmotic pressure difference. My own preference is for quarantine with copper treatment, which if properly carried out gets rid of both velvet and white spot harmlessly. Note that carbon filters must be turned off when copper medication is used, but

The selection of species for a marine tank is very important. Predators and prey animals of course cannot be mixed but care must also be taken to avoid species that will nip fins or constantly quarrel. If territorial fishes are included make sure there are more than enough suitable territories for all of them.

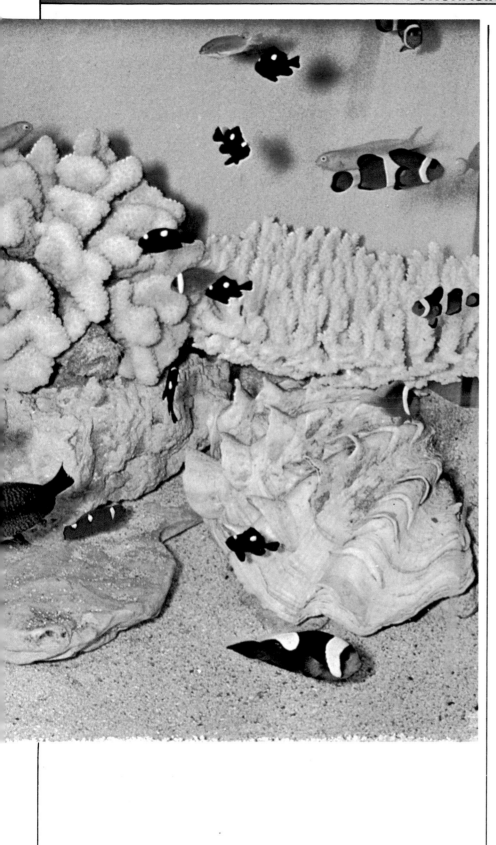

not biological filters.

It is possible to quarantine in a bare tank without filters of any kind, merely an airstone, if you can spare plenty of salt water. Part of the water and medication will have to be renewed at frequent intervals, say 25% or more every few days, but the method does allow good observation and control of dosage.

It is lucky that marine velvet *(Amyloodinium ocellatum)* and marine white spot *(Cryptocaryon irritans)* are both susceptible to copper treatment, as they are very common diseases and must always be suspected. They are also both highly contagious in the fish tank. A routine treatment for these two diseases is worth giving while the fishes are in quarantine. Other conditions are best treated as and if they crop up, as you cannot budget for every likely disease or parasite by prior treatment. If, after a period of two or better three weeks, the fishes seem healthy, they may be transferred to the aquarium.

When you begin to keep invertebrates, remember that they and the water they are in may convey disease to the tank. A period of quarantine *without* any treatment is wise. Many fish diseases will die off if without a host for two to three weeks or become so diluted that there is no great danger.

MIXING THE SPECIES

It is very likely that the choice of fishes you decide to put into the aquarium will depend on advice from friends, dealers or books. Also on what happens to catch your eye when going shopping. However, at least

Sometimes a fish must be quarantined. It is best to provide a separate tank without algae or invertebrates for observation or medication. Decorations should be minimal but enough to keep the fish from dashing about in panic. Illustration by John R. Quinn.

read the next chapter first, to avoid buying totally unsuitable species that fight, bully, grow too large, won't eat, and present various other difficulties, such as not usually living for long. There is a great variety of attractive, hardy, and peaceful species from which to choose, so don't ask for trouble.

There are some general facts about marine fishes that have to be learned, particularly about coral fishes. These are territorial in most cases and ready to defend their territory, especially against members of their own species or often of related species. Some live in communities, some are solitary. Don't be misled by the shoals or mixtures you see in the shop; these fishes have not had the chance to settle down and select a territory because they aren't offered one in a bare or nearly bare tank, or because they are so crowded that there is a continual melee. Don't buy "pairs" of fishes as is the custom of fresh water aquarists; single specimens or a group are usually safer. Buy a group only of a species that usually lives in groups.

Although most of the coral fishes don't share territories with members of the same species, except when forming mated pairs, they may be quite content to share them with totally unrelated ones. An angelfish that will beat the daylights out of another similar angel, may be happy sharing a coral head with some *Dascyllus* and perhaps a small eel. Luckily the territories of most fishes are quite limited—just a few feet from which they may rarely wander, and so in a really large aquarium it is possible to keep several related and otherwise belligerent specimens.

Some fishes, territory apart, are just too predatory or mean natured or both to be tolerated. Triggers often are, clown triggers *(Balistoides conspicillum)* usually being impossible to keep unless alone. Any of the groupers are suspect, being attractive when young and predatory later on. Others are too shy and starve if not kept among compatible tank mates. Seahorses *(Hippocampus* spp.) and mandarin fishes *Synchiropus* spp.) are examples that feed so slowly and delicately that other fishes will eat all the food before they have even started. Yet others are such specialized feeders that it is virtually impossible to keep them. Some of the chaetodons may accept only live coral, for example.

The Fishes

In this chapter we shall discuss the various families of fishes suitable for the marine aquarium and the merits and demerits of their members. First, however, something about classification. A **species** can be roughly defined as an interbreeding collection of creatures that appear to be of the same essential make-up. Nobody has in fact succeeded in defining a species entirely satisfactorily. However, we console ourselves by saying that we all know what we mean by the term! A **genus** is a step above a species, usually containing a group of species closely related to each other. A **family** is a collection of genera .... and so on.

A particular species usually has two names. A generic name and a specific name, both usually written in italics. *Amphiprion ocellaris* is the common anemone fish of the genus *Amphiprion.* Sometimes a fish has three names, that usually indicates that an original species has been split into two or more or that a fish thought to be of a separate species from another fish has now been classified with it - *Meiacanthus atrodorsalis oualanensis,* the canary blenny, now a subspecies of *Meiacanthus atrodorsalis,* the forktail blenny. Actually, I would normally write *M. a. atrodorsalis* the second time, as there is no need to repeat the generic name in full.

The most common anemonefish, *Amphiprion ocellaris*, is often called the Percula Clownfish even though there is a true *Amphiprion percula* (a rarer species). A better name for the common species would be Clown Anemonefish, a name by which it is also commonly known. This is an excellent beginner's fish although individuals from one geographic area may differ greatly in hardiness from those from another geographic area. Photo by Burkhard Kahl.

To complete the story, the name of the scientist who first classified the fish would be added to its scientific name - *Amphiprion ocellaris* Cuvier, but we often omit it in hobbyist books.

Why all this bother? Because only a fish's scientific (systematic) name identifies it, other names change with nations, localities, and times. Unfortunately scientific names are sometimes changed too, because of international agreement that the first person to describe a particular fish (or any creature) shall have the honor of naming it. So, if it is discovered later that the current name is not that originally given, it may have to be changed. Sometimes, as well, the same fish has been renamed by the same author (or another author) when caught somewhere else and something has to be done about that! Luckily, these changes seem to be much commoner among botanists than among zoologists, so we are relatively fortunate.

I shall now go on to discuss the merits of various commonly available species, grouping them into the *relatively cheap and hardy*, the *often not so cheap and less hardy ones,* finally some of the *often expensive and difficult fishes.* The two frequently go together anyway. The beginner is strongly advised to concentrate on the first group with an excursion or two into the second if he or she feels like it. The last group is included more as a warning than to incite buying!

Aquarium set-ups in which there are many invertebrates and few fishes such as the one shown here are gaining in popularity with the more advanced aquarists.
Photo by Chung.

GROUP 1

These fishes are usually inexpensive because they are easily caught and live well, sometimes because they are not all that attractive and so won't command high prices. They are easy to feed on most foods commonly offered.

The Blue-green Chromis, *Chromis viridis*, was formerly known as *Chromis caeruleus*. Illustration by Arita.

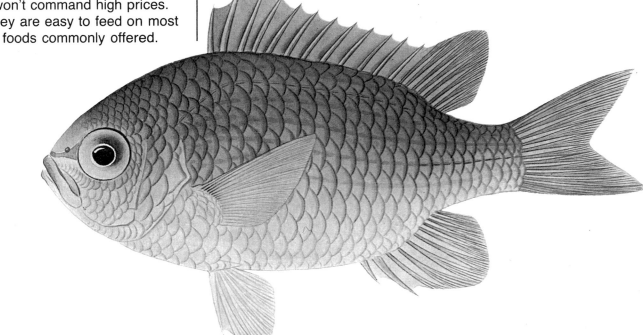

POMACENTRIDAE

This is a large family of hardy fishes found all over the tropics and includes the demoiselles or damselfishes and the anemone (clown) fishes. Many are territorial and fight with their own species. The rule is, therefore, one per tank, or a mated pair, except in large tanks. Some are schooling fishes and this is luckily true of the two *Chromis* described below:

Chromis viridis, the blue-green chromis and *C. cyanea,* the blue chromis, from the Indo-Pacific and mid-west Atlantic respectively, can be kept in schools of half-a-dozen even in a 30- or 40-gallon tank. Both are very good beginner's fishes and easy to keep. Although found in groups on the reefs of

Blue-green Chromis are among the commonest fishes on the reef. They are seen most often in large aggregations among the coral fronds in which they seek protection. Photo by Walter Deas.

Damselfishes school among the coral branches for protection while the butterflyfishes, which also use the coral for protection, utilize the corals and their associated fauna for food as well. Photo by Allan Power.

The Blue Chromis, *Chromis cyanea*, is the Caribbean version of the Indo-Pacific Blue-green Chromis. Photo by Dr. Gerald R. Allen.

the Indo-Pacific, *Pomacentrus coelestis,* the blue damselfish, is pugnacious in the aquarium and best kept singly. It is a beautiful fish, well worth keeping. *Chrysiptera cyanea* is a very similar fish often confused with *P. coelestis.* You will also find a number of other similar fishes offered from time to time, to which the same general remarks apply.

The *Dascyllus* species, characteristically black and white fishes, are pugnacious but very good fishes with which to start a tank. *D. aruanus,* the white-tailed damselfish and *D. melanurus,* the black-tailed damselfish, are otherwise similar. They are known to European aquarists as humbugs, because of their resemblance to popular black and white striped sweets. Both come from the Indo-Pacific in vast numbers, where they are almost as fond of anemones as the true anemone-fish. *D. trimaculatus,* the three-spot damselfish, grows rather large and is so aggressive that it is best avoided.

Chrysiptera cyanea, the sapphire devil and *Paraglyphidodon oxyodon,* the black velvet damselfish, both

The Blue Damselfish, *Pomacentrus coelestis*, as seen in their natural habitat at Santo, New Hebrides. Although they do well in a group here they are pugnacious and best kept singly in aquaria. Photo by Allan Power.

The Blue Damselfish often has a great deal of yellow color posteroventrally as seen in this individual. Photo by Dr. John E. Randall.

A Blue Devil, *Chrysiptera cyanea*, and a Blue-streak Devil, *Paraglyphidodon oxyodon*. Photo by Burkhard Kahl.

The White-tailed Damselfish, *Dascyllus aruanus*, in normal everyday coloration. Photo by Dr. Fujio Yasuda.

Aquarium spawning of damselfishes is not rare. Here a pair of White-tailed Damselfish, *Dascyllus aruanus*, are spawning on a branch of coral. Photo by Peter T. Jam.

▲ The Threespot Damselfish, *Dascyllus trimaculatus*, is not recommended as it becomes large and fierce. Photo by Burkhard Kahl.

A large anemone is shared by clownfish (*Amphiprion perideraion*) and damselfish (*Dascyllus trimaculatus*). Note the range in sizes of the Threespot Damselfish. Photo by Allan Power. ►

◄ The Blue-streak Damselfish is very attractive as a juvenile. The blue lines soon fade and the coloration becomes more somber. Photo by Dr. Herbert R. Axelrod.

◀ An aggregation of White-tailed Damselfish hovering above the protective coral as they select food particles from the drifting plankton. Photo by Allan Power.

▲
The White-tailed Damselfish, *Dascyllus aruanus*, as drawn by the Japanese artist Arita.

from the Philippines, are colorful species well worth having. They are related to *Abudefduf saxatilis,* the common "sergeant major" of worldwide tropical distribution. There are various other related species, mostly somewhat unattractive, but as tough as they come. Some are tide-pool species and can even stand rapid salinity and temperature changes.

The anemonefishes mostly belong to the genus *Amphiprion* and are a fascinating group. All live in and around large tropical anemones, often in groups that are the remains of original hatches of hundreds.

A common and inexpensive damselfish for the beginner is this Sergeant Major, *Abudefduf saxatilis.* ▼

Abudefduf saxatilis in its natural habitat on a Florida reef. Photo by Dr. Walter A. Starck II.

These are very young Sergeant Majors from Florida. It is not good to capture them this small as they probably will not survive. Older individuals are hardier. Photo by Dr. Herbert R. Axelrod.

There will typically be what appear to be a mother and father and a few young, but this is not so. What happens is that one mated pair grows up ahead of the others and by chemical means suppresses their growth. Only if one of the pair dies will another fish from the group grow and take the place of the female who, if the male dies, transforms to a male.

Amphiprion ocellaris, the clown anemonefish, and the best-known member of the genus, is imported in vast numbers. However, it is not the toughest species and needs rather careful handling when first imported if losses are to be avoided. It is a school fish, although not an open water one, being always near its home anemone. This is most commonly a *Stoichactis,* but it will accept *Radianthus, Tealia,* and others (all large tropical anemones). The yellow and white typical of *A. ocellaris* from most areas is replaced by orange and blue with heavy black borders in the supposedly separate species, the very handsome *A. percula.* However, intermediate forms found around northern Australia and New Guinea, even practically black forms, make one wonder.

A. clarkii, the yellow-tailed anemonefish, widely distributed in tropical seas, is another, chunkier, three-barred fish. It is attractive, tougher than *A. ocellaris,* and grows larger (up to 6″ as against 3″ or so). It looks nicest at about 1½″ and grows quite slowly, even when on its own.

A. frenatus, the red anemonefish, has only one bar, on the head. *A. ephippium,* the saddle anemonefish, has none,

The common Clown Anemonefish, *Amphiprion ocellaris*, does best when kept with an anemone. Pet shops that sell the anemonefish normally will have suitable anemones for sale as well. Photo by Burkhard Kahl.

This is the rarer Percula Clownfish, *Amphiprion percula*. The black areas help in identification but may not always be so obvious as in this individual. Photo by Dr. Fujio Yasuda.

This *Amphiprion percula* has the black areas much reduced and it is more difficult to distinguish from the Clown Anemonefish, *Amphiprion ocellaris*. Photo by Dr. Gerald R. Allen.

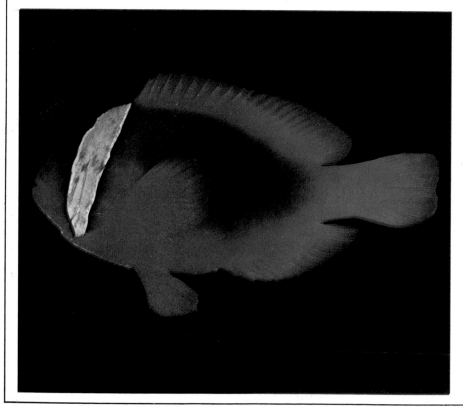

The Red or Tomato Clownfish, *Amphiprion frenatus*, is another favorite of marine aquarists and is recommended for beginners. Photo by Dr. John E. Randall.

►

Like the other clownfishes this *Amphiprion frenatus* feels more secure when an anemone is present in the tank. Large, showy anemones of the genus *Condylactus* are often preferred. Photo by K. H. Choo.

Spawnings are not infrequent. This Red Anemonefish spawned next to the anemone with the pinkish orange eggs visible just below the fish. Both parents usually stand guard over the clutch of eggs. Photo by Dr. Herbert R. Axelrod.

Anemonefishes can be kept without anemones but there should be caves or other protected areas where they can hide when danger threatens. This is *Amphiprion frenatus*. Photo by Dr. D. Terver, Nancy ▼ Aquarium, France.

An unusual example of Clark's Anemonefish, *Amphiprion clarkii*, above the anemone. A more normal colored individual is below. Photo by Pierre Laboute.

The dark form of Clark's Anemonefish, *Amphiprion clarkii*. These two individuals were photographed by Dr. Herbert R. Axelrod in the Maldive Islands.

◄ These Clark's Anemonefish eggs are well protected by one of the parent fish as well as their proximity to the stinging tentacles of the anemone. Photo by Jan Carlen.

Frightened anemonefish nestle among the tentacles of their anemone. When the danger passes they again move out into the water column to feed. This is *Amphiprion clarkii*. Photo by Dr. Herbert R. Axelrod. ▼

▲The Skunk-striped Anemonefish, *Amphiprion akallopisos*, does not have the vertical pale stripe on the nape and operculum. Photo by Dr. D. Terver, Nancy Aquarium, France.

◄

Amphiprion perideraion is known as the False Skunk-striped Anemonefish. This is a female. Photo by Dr. Herbert R. Axelrod.

The male False Skunk-striped Anemonefish has reddish orange stripes on the upper and lower edges of his caudal fin. Photo by Dr. Herbert R. Axelrod.
◄

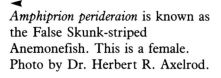

Usually a whole "family" of anemonefishes will inhabit a single anemone. Here some *Amphiprion perideraion* pick at the oral opening of their anemone for bits of food. Photo by Allan Power.

A pair of False Skunk-striped Anemonefish that was raised in captivity at Nancy Aquarium. Many fishes are quite long-lived if provided with the proper conditions. Photo by Dr. D. Terver, Nancy Aquarium, France.

but does have a black saddle. Both are rather aggressive and best kept singly. Various other anemonefishes are more peaceful and easier to handle, such as *A. akallopisos,* the skunk anemonefish and *A. perideraion,* the false skunk anemonefish, which has a stripe on the head as well as on the back. Both are from the Indo-Pacific and easy to keep in batches with an anemone.

A very attractive anemonefish belongs to the genus *Premnas,* which has one or more spines beneath each eye. *P. biaculeatus,* the spine-cheeked anemonefish, from the Indo-Pacific, is velvety red with three narrow white stripes and grows to about 6". It must taste delicious to other fishes, as they are very prone to nipping its fins, so that it is advisable to see that it is a dominant fish in the tank. It is also pugnacious, when adult, towards others of the same species. Most species of anemonefish have been bred in the aquarium, some commercially, and although it is unlikely that you will raise any young, it is not uncommon for them to lay batches of eggs on a shell or coral in the tank.

The most distinctive anemonefish is this *Premnas biaculeatus.* It is sometimes called the Maroon Clownfish because of its color. Like the other anemonefishes it prefers to have an anemone close at hand for safety. Photo by Roger Steene.

The scientific name *biaculeatus* means "two-spined". The two spines can easily be seen in this photograph. The common name Spine-cheeked Anemonefish also refers to this distinctive character. Photo by Dr. Herbert R. Axelrod.

The Spine-cheeked Anemonefish is quite variable in color and pattern. The width of the stripes on the head and body may vary from very narrow to quite wide. Photo by Dr. Herbert R. Axelrod.

The Bluestreak Cleaner Wrasse is a full-time cleaner. This means it feeds almost exclusively on the parasites and other material it removes from other fishes. Photo of *Labroides dimidiatus* by K. H. Choo.

Juvenile *Coris gaimard* are commonly called the Clown Wrasse because of the pattern of black-bordered white blotches on the head and body. Photo by Dr. John E. Randall.

Coris gaimard juveniles are hard to capture as they dive into the sandy substrate when pursued. They may pop up again several feet away only to disappear again if the danger still threatens. Photo by Roger Steene.

A number of other wrasses are cleaners when young, as indeed are a lot of young fishes. The genus *Coris* is a good example. *C. gaimard*, the red labrid, is also a good example of color changes. As a juvenile it has a brilliant orange-red body with white spots or bars, but when adult it is blue-striped and spotted, in a quite different pattern, on a reddish-brown body. Other *Coris* species undergo equally spectacular changes. Some grow far too large—up to four feet long.

Wrasses that are both attractive and stay reasonably small include two old favorites, the rainbow wrasse,

This *Coris gaimard* is changing from its juvenile pattern to the adult pattern. This change is quite dramatic. Photo by Dr. Herbert R. Axelrod.

Aquarists consider *Coris gaimard* a desirable inhabitant for their aquaria even though it occasionally disappears from view into the sand. Photo by K. H. Choo.

Wrasses are notoriously poor photographic models. This *Thalassoma lunare* is being held in place for the camera. Photo by Dr. Herbert R. Axelrod.

Adult male *Thalassoma lunare* at a depth of about 20 feet at Madang, New Guinea. This 5-inch individual is almost fully grown. Photo by Dr. Gerald R. allen.

Thalassoma amblycephalum, and the moon wrasse or lyretail wrasse, *T. lunare.* Both grow only to about 6″. Others are *Gomphosus varius,* the beakfish, with bright green males and brown females and *Macropharyngodon meleagris,* the leopard wrasse, with a green and brown spotted body.

The parrotfishes, *Scarus* species, family Scaridae, come in various striking colors. Most don't grow too fast or too big in the aquarium, and have the weird habit of secreting a cocoon of mucus at night. Parrotfishes are vegetarians, but many wrasses are fond of small crustaceans and other meaty food.

A colorful super male *Thalassoma amblycephalum*. This individual sustained some damage to its lower jaw, possibly during capture or during the acclimation process to captive living. Photo by Dr. Fujio Yasuda.

A young male *Thalassoma amblycephalum* and the quite different juvenile phase (insert). Females and some males retain the juvenile pattern into the adult stage while the remaining males become super males with a completely different pattern. Photos by Dr. Herbert R. Axelrod at Mombasa.

Sexual dimorphism is common in wrasses causing many problems with their correct nomenclature. This is a female Green Bird Wrasse, *Gomphosus varius*. Photo by Dr. Fujio Yasuda.

The male Green Bird Wrasse is obviously the one that inspired the common name. This individual is casting a wary eye on two of its tankmates, a *Thalassoma* and a *Paracanthurus hepatus*. Photo by Dr. Herbert R. Axelrod.

The prolonged snout of *Gomphosus varius* is unusual among wrasses but not unusual among fishes. Long-snouted species appear in a number of different fish families, apparently enabling them to reach into coral crevices for food that short-snouted species cannot reach. Photo by Dr. Fujio Yasuda.

This colorful *Macropharyngodon bipartitus* male was photographed in its natural habitat in the Gulf of Aqaba, Red Sea. It is about 4½ inches in total length. Photo by Dr. Victor G. Springer.

Macropharyngodon choati is a relatively recently described species from the east coast of Australia. This adult is approximately 80 mm standard length and was collected at Byron Bay, New South Wales. Photo by Rudie Kuiter.

Two very young individuals of *Macropharyngodon choati* that came from North Solitary Island, New South Wales. The specimen above is 10 mm, the one below 20 mm standard length. Photos by Rudie Kuiter.

This 40 mm long individual is developing the adult pattern. Not many wrasses have such a direct development of pattern as this species. Photo by Rudie Kuiter at Byron Bay, New South Wales.

Macropharyngodon meleagris ornatus at Christmas Island, Indian Ocean. Photo by Roger Steene.

Macropharyngodon meleagris meleagris from the Marshall Islands. Photo by Dr. John E. Randall.

Juvenile (20 mm S.L.) *Macropharyngodon meleagris* from New South Wales. Photo by Rudie Kuiter.

Macropharyngodon meleagris ornatus from Ambon Island in the East Indies. Photo by Dr. Gerald R. Allen.

A variety of parrotfish species. Upper left: *Scarus frenatus*. Upper right: *Scarus* sp. Lower left: *Scarus ghobban*. Lower right: *Scarus gibbus*. Photos by Michio Goto, Marine Life Documents.

Many parrotfishes sleep encased in a mucous envelope which affords them some protection from nocturnal predators. This is *Scarus gibbus* with its coccoon. Photo by Michio Goto, *Marine Life Documents*.

A female Caribbean parrotfish, *Scarus iserti*, sleeping in its mucous coccoon. The envelope starts out completely transparent but soon becomes covered with silt. Photo by Dr. Walter A. Starck II.

A super male *Scarus vetula*. Parrotfishes have spawning patterns similar to those of the wrasses, including pair spawning involving super males and group spawning involving similarly patterned males and females. Photo by Dr. Patrick L. Colin.

GOBIIDAE AND BLENNIIDAE

Fishes you will rarely find conspicuous in a dealer's tanks are the gobies and blennies, except perhaps for the neon goby, *Gobiosoma oceanops,* a cleaner. They are characteristically small; bottom-dwelling fishes that often cost little and live well. The Catalina goby, *Lythrypnus dalli,* from the island of that name in California, is a real beauty,although rather tiny at 1¼" long, with a bright red body and blue bars. It can take quite cool water, too. *Gobiodon citrinus,* the lemon goby, is an upright flattened fish that wedges itself in coral; it is about 2" long.

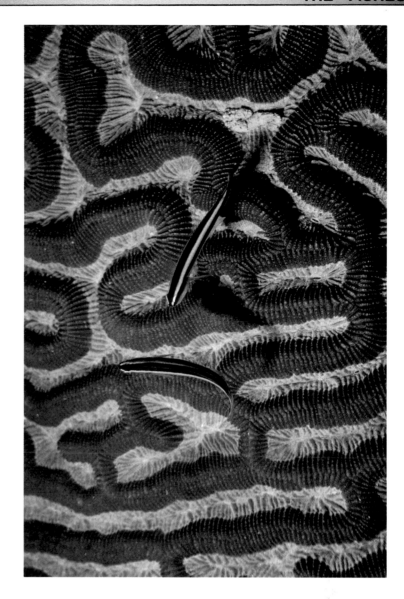

Neon Gobies, *Gobiosoma oceanops*, can be seen on the surface of several different corals. But they are never far from a hole into which they can quickly disappear. Photo by Dr. Patrick L. Colin.

In an aquarium Neon Gobies should be provided with cave-like shelters. Coral rock is good for this purpose. Photo by Dr. Patrick L. Colin.

An egg-laden female *Gobiosoma oceanops* following a male into his PVC tube nest. Photo by Dr. Patrick L. Colin.

The male Neon Goby keeps his nest clean of any debris. This individual was caught in the act of spitting out some sand that he removed from the nest. Photo by Dr. Patrick L. Colin.

When all is satisfactory the male stands guard over the eggs. At this time he becomes very aggressive and will even attack an aquarist's finger if placed too close. Photo by Dr. Patrick L. Colin.

▲ The Catalina Goby, *Lythrypnus dalli*, is one of the most colorful native West Coast fishes. It is protected by law so that aquarists will not be able to obtain aquarium specimens. Photo by Ken Lucas, Steinhart Aquarium.

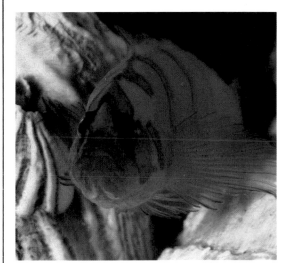

◄
A head-on view of the beautiful Catalina Goby. This species is also known by the common name Bluebanded Goby for obvious reasons, but there are other red-orange gobies with blue bands which may cause confusion if that common name were used. Photo by Burkhard Kahl.

Lythrypnus dalli in its natural habitat. Photo by Al Engasser.

One of the most spectacular of the Mediterranean blennies is the Carmine Blenny, *Lipophrys nigriceps*. Photo by Gerhard Marcuse.

Some of the North Atlantic and Mediterranean blennies are spectacular, although not usually available elsewhere. The carmine blenny, *Lipophrys nigriceps;* the peacock blenny, *Salaria pavo;* and the horned blenny, *Parablennius tentacularis* are good examples. Many blennies have little horns on the head, but *P. tentacularis* has almost antlers. Both gobies and blennies guard their eggs and many species have been bred in the aquarium.

The Carmine Blenny inhabits rock crevices down to a depth of about 20 feet. Photo by Gunter Spies.

The male Peacock Blenny, *Salaria pavo*, develops this bump on its head. Photo by H. Hansen, Aquarium Berlin.

The female *Salaria pavo* have a more normally shaped head. The spot behind the eye may be a false eye to misdirect attacks. Photo by Stanislav Frank.

Many blennies have head tentacles but *Parablennius tentacularis* has long and conspicuous ones as can be seen here. Photo by H. Hansen, Aquarium Berlin.

Blennies have reduced pelvic fins. This *Parablennius tentacularis* is resting on them as it eyes the photographer warily. Photo by H. Hansen, Aquarium Berlin.

A dark phase of the Horned Blenny, *Parablennius tentacularis*. The tentacles are shorter in this individual but more branched. Photo by Stanislav Frank.

BALISTIDAE (BALISTINAE)

The triggerfishes are so named because of a locking device on the dorsal fin that "triggers" it into a stiff, erect spine, fixing the fish in position in a crevice in coral. Most of them are large and aggressive, but I include a few here that are tolerable and very hardy. They eat practically anything, but in nature feed mostly on small crustaceans, sea urchins and mollusks, hence are not suited to aquaria containing invertebrates.

Odonus niger, the black triggerfish, that is often blue

The Black Triggerfish, *Odonus niger*, should not be kept with timid tank-mates. It grows to a length of about 8 inches. Photo by Dr. Herbert R. Axelrod.

The color of the Black Triggerfish varies considerably. It can be blackish to greenish to bluish and all shades between. This individual is posing for a cleaner wrasse visible on its tail. Photo by Burkhard Kahl.

rather than black, is a handsome and reasonably peaceful fish, but still should not be kept with timid companions. It comes from the Indo-Pacific and Red Sea and grows to around 8″. Another black trigger, often with only black fins however, is *Melichthys indicus,* but it grows too big, about 20″, and isn't always very peaceful. *Rhinecanthus aculeatus,* the Picasso trigger from Hawaii and the Indo-Pacific also enjoys a native name often longer than itself: Humu-humu-nuku-nuku-a-puaa. It does however grow to about 12″, but 1″—2″ specimens are favorites—very pretty and non-aggressive. If you get one, don't feed it too enthusiastically!

A frontal view of the Black Triggerfish showing the pattern of lines running from the eyes to the mouth and the red teeth. Photo by Burkhard Kahl.

Odonus niger. Photo Michio Goto, *Marine Life Documents.*

The Humu-humu-nuku-nuku-a-puaa or Picasso Triggerfish grows to about a foot in length but small individuals are aquarium favorites. Photo by Dr. Herbert R. Axelrod.

81

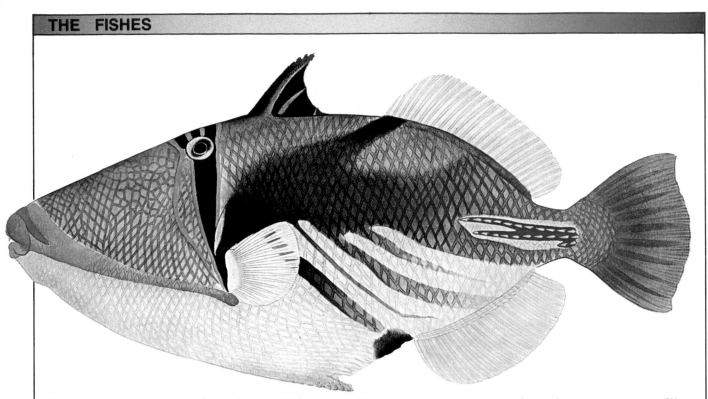

The complicated pattern of this Picasso Triggerfish, *Rhinecanthus aculeatus*, gave rise to its common name. Illustration by Arita.

The juvenile Picasso Triggerfish has much the same pattern as the adult. Photo by Dr. Herbert R. Axelrod of a juvenile specimen from the Maldive Islands.

Melichthys indicus is also highly variable in color but always has the bright white lines at the bases of the dorsal and anal fins. Photo by H. Hansen, Aquarium Berlin.

The dark phase of *Melichthys indicus*. Note that all three individuals on this page have black dorsal and anal fins. Photo by Dr. Herbert R. Axelrod.

In this lighter phase the pattern of the caudal fin is more noticeable. Like other triggerfishes this species should not be kept with timid fishes. Photo by Klaus Paysan.

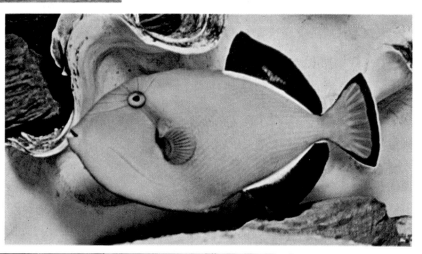

APOGONIDAE

These are the cardinalfishes, quite hardy but with the one drawback that they like live food, will learn to eat frozen or fresh foods, but rarely can be weaned onto dry foods. They are said to be mouthbrooders (raising the eggs and the young in the mouth for a period after hatching). Local American species are *Apogon binotatus* and *A. maculatus,* both red and attractive. Many other species come from the Indo-Pacific, the commonest being *Sphaeramia nematoptera,* a chunky, beautiful fish, growing slowly to about 4". Unlike many cardinals, it is not shy or nocturnal.

Apogon binotatus is one of the Caribbean species that is commonly available to aquarists. This attractive individual was photographed at night at a depth of about 30 feet in the Bahama Islands. Photo by Dr. Patrick L. Colin.

Sphaeramia orbicularis, shown here, is often confused with the more colorful *S. nematoptera,* the Pajama Cardinalfish. Illustration by Tomita.

Apogon binotatus exhibiting the two characteristic vertical bands that gave it its scientific name. Photo by Dr. Patrick L. Colin.

One of the favorites from the Caribbean is *Apogon maculatus*. It is bright red with a black spot here and there for contrast. Photo by Gerhard Marcuse.

The Pajama Cardinalfish is one of the few cardinalfishes that will stay out in the open during the day. Most other cardinalfishes are nocturnal. Photo by Dr. Gerald R. Allen.

Two different species of cardinalfishes (*Apogon maculatus* with the two spots and *Apogon pseudomaculatus* with the spot and bar) using a long-spined sea urchin for protection. Photo by Dr. Walter A. Starck II.

The black spots in this *Apogon maculatus* have faded but the bright red color that inspired the name cardinalfishes is quite strong. Photo by Dr. Walter A. Starck II.

TETRAODONTIDAE (CANTHIGASTERINAE)

Pufferfishes are able to inflate themselves with water as a defense mechanism, like the even more spectacular porcupinefishes (Diodontidae) that are covered with spines and look very formidable when inflated. Both make good aquarium fishes, are hardy, and ready to eat almost anything. *Canthigaster margaritata,* the Red Sea sharp-nosed puffer, actually from many tropical areas, and *C. valentini,* the sharp-nosed puffer, are favorites. *C. coronata,* the Crown Toby , again from many other places, is an oddity that sits at an angle in the water with a pinched-in tail. Most puffer species can inflict painful bites, despite their small size.

Canthigaster margaritata, the Red Sea Sharp-nosed Puffer, is hardy and will eat a variety of foods in captivity. Photo by Dr. Herbert R. Axelrod.

Bennett's Sharp-nosed Puffer, *Canthigaster bennetti*, is one of the more common sharp-nosed puffers available to aquarists. Photo by Dr. Shih-Chieh Shen.

The green eyes and radiating stripes extending back from the eye are seen in several species of sharpnosed puffers. This is *Canthigaster valentini*. Photo by Dr. Herbert R. Axelrod.

Canthigaster valentini in its natural surroundings. Photo by Michio Goto, *Marine Life Documents*.

The Crown Toby, *Canthigaster coronata*, resembles *C. valentini* in general pattern but on closer observation differences can be seen. For example look at the extent ventrally of the middle dark bars. Photo by Burkhard Kahl.

GROUP 2

We come now to an extensive group of fishes that are in general less easy to manage than those in Group 1 and are often decidedly more expensive. Of course, prices vary and many depend on where you are; Pacific fishes cost more in America than in Australia and it is very much *vice versa* with Atlantic fishes.

A juvenile Queen Angelfish, *Holacanthus ciliaris*. Juveniles of the Queen and Blue Angelfishes are very difficult to distinguish. Photo by Dr. John E. Randall.

One of the differences is the curved light body stripe in this Queen Angelfish. It is straight in the Blue Angelfish. Photo by Dr. Herbert R. Axelrod.

This adult Queen Angelfish is usually too big for average home aquaria, attaining lengths of 10 to 12 inches. Photo by Dr. John E. Randall.

Holacanthus clarionensis (adult). Photo by Dr. Herbert R. Axelrod.

Holacanthus clarionensis (juvenile). Photo by Al Engasser.

Holacanthus ciliaris (adult). Photo by Dr. Patrick L. colin.

Holacanthus isabelita (adult). Photo by Dr. John E. Randall.

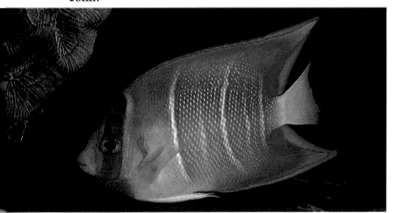

Holacanthus ciliaris (juvenile). Photo by Dr. Walter A. Starck II.

Holacanthus isabelita (juvenile). Photo by Dr. Patrick L. Colin.

Holacanthus passer (adult). Photo by Alex Kerstitch.

Holacanthus passer (juvenile). Photo by Alex Kerstitch.

Small juvenile *Holacanthus tricolor* have a blue-ringed black spot within the black blotch. Photo by Charles Arneson.

As the fish grows the black blotch expands to cover much of the body of the Rock Beauty. Photo by Dr. Gerald R. Allen.

The Rock Beauty is a good beginner's fish if it is provided with a proper diet.

POMACANTHIDAE

The angelfishes, like the wrasses, undergo color changes as they grow up, often so profound that you would never recognize them as belonging to the same species. The smaller species grow to only a few inches in length and could almost have been included in Group 1, but they are mostly expensive and at least a shade more difficult to keep. The larger angels get quite big and many are touchy as to water conditions and general care. They also tolerate each other poorly, even those of different species. Again, the smaller species are more docile and can often be kept together. A large specimen of almost any of the other species will usually tolerate quite small specimens, even of his own species, or a mate. All angels have spines on the gill covers and can do severe damage to another fish.

The genus *Holacanthus* includes popular Atlantic angels, but is represented in the Pacific as well. The queen angelfish *(H. ciliaris)* has blue bars when young but blue borders later, and grows to about 18″. The blue angelfish *(H. isabelita)* is very similar and interbreeds with the queen angelfish in nature. The rock beauty *(H. tricolor)* merely darkens as it grows, from yellow with a blue-edged black spot on its back to nearly black all over. Given algae to eat, it is tougher than the others and a good beginner's fish.

The genus *Centropyge* includes the pygmy angels, from the Pacific mostly, but is represented by a few Atlantic species, of which *C. argi*, the cherubfish, is best known, but is

As the Rock Beauty grows it develops a filament on the end of the dorsal fin and eventually the anal fin as well. Photo by Arend van den Nieuwenhuizen.

The wrasse, *Bodianus rufus*, seems to object to the presence of the angelfish, *Holacanthus tricolor*. The dispute could be over food among other things.

The photos on this page represent a sequence in the spawning behavior of the Rock Beauty, *Holacanthus tricolor*. The pair will swim up in the water column, engage in nuzzling activity, and eventually release sperm and eggs. All photos by Charles Arneson except that at lower left, which is by Dr. Patrick L. Colin.

rare and expensive, living in deep waters. Pygmy angels grow to 3″ or 4″ characteristically and are good to keep. The Pacific species are naturally not cheap in the U.S.A. as they mostly come from the western regions, but Hawaii supplies *C. fisheri,* Fisher's angelfish, that is a beauty, but also rather rare; *C. loriculus,* the flame angelfish, another beauty—as in fact they nearly all are; and *C. potteri,* the russet angelfish, the commonest of the three.

The Pacific pygmy angels are all worth having, except for *C. bicolor,* the blue-and-gold angelfish, that besides being expensive is difficult to keep. It also grows quite large, but that would be the least of your problems. *C. bispinosus,* the dusky angelfish, lives well and is most attractive; so is *C. flavissimus,* the lemonpeel angelfish, with its bright yellow body and blue markings. *C. heraldi,* the golden angelfish, is just yellow with a brownish dappling on fins and head.

The genus *Pomacanthus,* containing many large angels, is widely distributed in tropical seas. Juveniles are characteristically striped, blue and white, or black and yellow. Adults are quite different from the young and the transformation is intriguing to watch if the fish lives long enough, as many now do. From the Atlantic come *P. arcuatus* and *P. paru,* the gray and French angelfishes respectively. They are very similar, juveniles having black and yellow stripes, adults becoming gray-brown or blackish, with golden flecks in *P. paru.* Both grow to 1½ or 2 feet. *P. arcuatus* is the bigger.

Centropyge fisheri is one of Hawaii's endemic angelfishes. It is relatively uncommon and not brightly colored but still always welcome by marine aquarists. Photo by Dr. Gerald R. Alleen.

Centropyge fisheri from Molokini, Hawaiian Islands. Photo by Dr. John E. Randall.

One of the most brightly colored of the pygmy angelfishes is this Flame Angelfish, *Centropyge loriculus.* Photo by Dr. Dwayne Reed.

A Flame Angelfish presents itself to be cleaned by a pair of cleaner shrimp, *Lysmata grabhami*. The long white antennae of the shrimp are a signal that the fish can be cleaned at that spot.

The Flame Angelfish is not discriminatory when it comes to cleaners. This individual has sought the services of the cleaner wrasse *Labroides dimidiatus*.

The commonest Hawaiian endemic pygmy angelfish is *Centropyge potteri*. The Russet or Potter's Angelfish is beautifully patterned in orange and blue. Photo by Gene Wolfsheimer.
►

The Blue-and-gold Angelfish, *Centropyge bicolor*, does poorly in captivity. Perhaps the problem is diet but so far nobody has been able to determine what is wrong. Photo by Dr. Gerald R. Allen. ▼

Centropyge potteri in its natural habitat among the corals of Hawaii. This individual is about 3 inches in length. Photo by Dr. Gerald R. Allen.

Centropyge bicolor is one of the larger pygmy angelfishes but mostly small individuals find their way to pet shops. Perhaps the smaller fish are a bit hardier than the larger ones. Photo by Allan Power.

The Dusky Angelfish, *Centropyge bispinosus*, is not only attractive but also stands up fairly well in captivity. The relative proportions of the blue and orange colors differ in different individuals, the more orange ones said to be females. Photo by Dr. Herbert R. Axelrod.

The juvenile Lemonpeel, *Centropyge flavissimus*, sports a large blue-rimmed black spot on its side. This quickly disappears with growth. Photo by Allan Power.

Adult *Centropyge flavissimus* are a bright yellow accented with powder blue, this latter color particularly noticeable on the gill cover and cheek spine. Photo by Dr. Herbert R. Axelrod.

Lemonpeels are fairly hardy if provided with a proper diet. Hiding places should be provided and all pygmy angelfishes prefer to retire to a secure place in the tank when frightened. Photo by Dr. D. Terver, Nancy Aquarium.

The Golden or Herald's Angelfish, *Centropyge heraldi*, has the same golden color as the Lemonpeel but without the blue markings. Photo by Dr. Fujio Yasuda.

A constant part of the pattern is a longitudinal band through the anal fin. Sexual dimorphism is manifested by a blotchy dark head in the male. This is a female. Photo by K. H. Choo.

The Lemonpeel, *Centropyge flavissimus,* in its natural habitat keeping a wary eye on the photographer. It can disappear into the reef in a flash but will usually peek out from a nearby hole again within a few minutes. Photo by Allan Power.

Only two pygmy angelfishes are known from the tropical Western Atlantic. This is the more common species, *Centropyge argi*. Photo by Arend van den Nieuwenhuizen.

A Cherubfish, *Centropyge argi*, in its natural habitat where it can dash into a cave and disappear from view very quickly. Photo Charles Arneson.

French and Gray Angelfishes are difficult to distinguish when in their juvenile stages. This is a juvenile Gray Angelfish, *Pomacanthus arcuatus,* because the edge of the caudal fin has a broad clear or whitish edge. Photo by Dr. Herbert R. Axelrod.

An adult Gray Angelfish, *Pomacanthus arcuatus,* poses for the cleaner goby *Gobiosoma illecebrosum.* Photo by Carl Roessler at Islas Rosarios, Colombia.

A smaller version of the French Angelfish. Photo by Douglas Faulkner.

Juvenile angelfishes are at their best at this size. They still have full color but are large enough to withstand the rigors of captivity. This is a young French Angelfish. Photo by Arend van den Nieuwenhuizen.

The French Angelfish can be identified head-on by the wishbone-shaped yellow marking around its mouth. The Gray Angelfish has the same marking but in addition has a vertical stripe crossing the mouth.

A French Angelfish, *Pomacanthus paru*, assuming an unusually awkward position to allow the cleaner wrasses better access to its body. What is interesting is that these wrasses (*Labroides dimidiatus*) are Indo-Pacific cleaners but are immediately recognized by even this Caribbean species. Photo by Arend van den Nieuwenhuizen.

Juveniles of the French Angelfish, *Pomacanthus paru*, are themselves part-time cleaners, this one searching for edible material around the erected dorsal fin spines of the Bank Butterflyfish, *Chaetodon sedentarius*. Photo by Klaus Paysan.

This French Angelfish, *Pomacanthus paru*, is in an intermediate stage between juvenile and adult. The yellow stripes of the juvenile are plainly evident but the yellow edging of the scales, which is an adult color character, can also be seen. Another evidence of approaching adulthood in this individual are the prolongations into filaments of the dorsal and anal fins. Aquarists prefer the French Angelfish over the Gray Angelfish because the former retains the juvenile characters longer than the latter. Photo by Conrad Limbaugh.

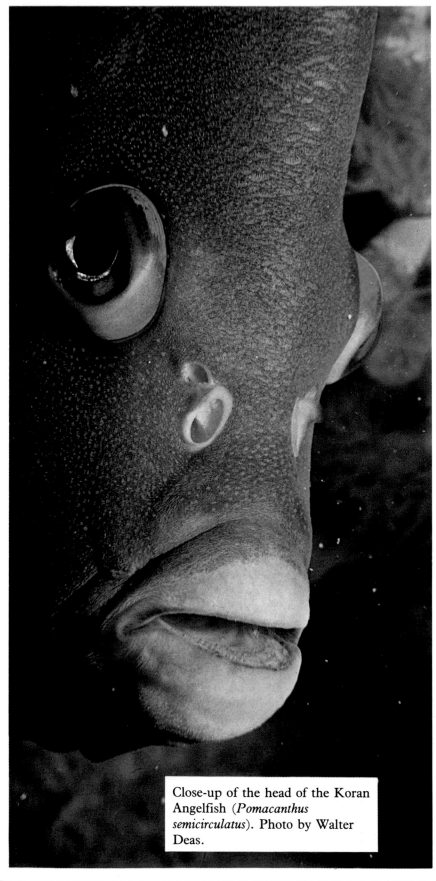

Close-up of the head of the Koran Angelfish (*Pomacanthus semicirculatus*). Photo by Walter Deas.

Most Pacific angels in the genus start off as blue and white juveniles, easily confused with one another in some cases. In the aquarium they take about 2 years to change to the adult pattern, but probably do so more rapidly in nature. *P. semicirculatus,* the Koran angelfish, with concentric white semicircular, narrow bands is a good fish to start with, as easy to raise as any of them. *P. imperator,* the emperor angelfish, has complete circular markings when young, later becoming a most impressive adult with blue and yellow horizontal stripes. *Euxiphipops navarchus,* the blue-girdled angelfish, has vertical juvenile white strips, later becoming an equally handsome adult with blue patches and dots on an orange background. The three represent approximately three stages in difficulty of rearing, *E.*

Pomacanthus semicirculatus adult in its natural habitat. Photo by Pierre Laboute.

➤

A subadult *Pomacanthus semicirculatus* still with remnants of the juvenile pattern. Photo by Dr. Fujio Yasuda.

A Koran Angelfish being cleaned by *Labroides dimidiatus*. Photo by Allan Power.

A young *Pomacanthus semicirculatus*. Photo by Gene Wolfsheimer.

A Koran Angelfish still in juvenile dress but older than the above individual. Photo by Dr. Fujio Yasuda.

Several species of angelfishes have similar juveniles in which there is a dark body with a pattern of white lines. The upper two photos show juveniles of *Pomacanthus imperator*. The one with the complete circle posteriorly is more normal. The Koran Angelfish *(Pomacanthus semicirculatus)* is seen at the lower right with the Arabic markings on the tail, and the Yellow-faced Angelfish *(Euxiphipops xanthometopon)* with the yellow pectoral fins at the lower left. In this last species the adult color pattern is starting to show through. Photos by Dr. D. Terver, Nancy Aquarium.

A juvenile Emperor Angelfish, *Pomacanthus imperator*. This species does well in captivity and is very popular with aquarists. Photo by Dr. Fujio Yasuda.

An Emperor Angelfish that has attained much of the adult pattern but still retains remnants of the white lines of the juvenile. Photo by Dr. Fujio Yasuda.

Adult Emperor Angelfish can be seen in the two photos below. The one on the left is in its natural habitat. Photos by Dr. Herbert R. Axelrod.

An early illustration of the young of the Emperor Angelfish. This fairly accurate rendition is from Bleeker's *Atlas Ichthyologique*.

The small mouths of the angelfishes mean small food size. The Emperor Angelfish will usually accept things like brine shrimp, bloodworms, chopped clam, prawn, and boiled spinach. Photo by K. H. Choo.

▲
A juvenile Blue-girdled Angelfish, *Euxiphipops navarchus*, in its natural habitat. Photographed at New Britain by Roger Lubbock.

Euxiphipops navarchus is not as hardy as some of the other marine angelfishes and is sometimes difficult to feed. Photo by Earl Kennedy.
◄

The Blue-girdled Angelfish loses its juvenile color pattern at an early age. Fortunately the adult pattern is just as attractive. Photo by Earl Kennedy.
►

Adult angelfishes usually can be kept in a community tank situation with species of similar temperament. Photo by Earl Kennedy.

navarchus often presenting feeding problems. With a bit of experience, try any of the other available Pacific angels except *Pygoplytes diacanthus,* which has proved almost unmanageable even in expert hands, living at best for a few months to a year and dying usually of slow starvation.

It is a good rule to avoid very young or adult fishes when making a purchase, as both may prove difficult to feed. This is very true of the angelfishes. When tiny, they are hard to rear. At 1½″ to 2″ they mostly eat small live or deep-frozen foods readily and even dry foods in some cases. As wild-caught adults they have become accustomed to their often specialist diets. These may be sponges, corals, or other exotic items difficult to provide and difficult from which to wean them.

A Blue-girdled Angelfish being cleaned by a Cleaner Wrasse, *Labroides dimidiatus.* Photo by Gunter Spies.

A young Regal Angelfish, *Pygoplites diacanthus*. The Regal Angelfish does not undergo the dramatic color and pattern changes of its close relatives. Unfortunately, this species is very difficult to keep, living at best for a few months to a year. Photo by Michael Gilroy.

An adult Regal Angelfish swimming among the corals in the Red Sea. Photo by Helmut Debelius.

Pygoplites diacanthus is wide-ranging in the Indo-Pacific region. It inhabits reef areas where it can disappear quickly when danger threatens. Photo by Guy van den Bossche.

CHAETODONTIDAE

The chaetodonts, or marine butterflyfishes, provide a wide range of species varying from moderately easy, if you take good care of them, to practically impossible to keep. They do best at high temperatures, around 80°-84°F, rather high specific gravity, around 1.023 at 80°F, corresponding to 1.026 at 60°F, and good aeration and water movement. As with the angels, they are best bought at a medium juvenile size or somewhat larger, say 2″-3″, kept as defined above, later gently switched to the more usual 75°-77°F and 1.022 specific gravity if desired. Live foods or at least high-grade frozen foods are important, particularly at first. Some will only eat if tricked by tucking finely chopped clam or beef heart into coral, and with luck will later take other foods.

There are few unattractive chaetodons, so start off with ones you are most likely to keep successfully. These are likely to be *C. auriga,* the threadfin butterflyfish (also called filament butterflyfish); *C. capistratus,* the foureye butterflyfish; *C. ephippium,* the black-blotched butterflyfish; *C. melannotus,* the black-backed butterflyfish; *C. lunula,* the raccoon butterfly-fish; *C. rafflesi,* the latticed butterflyfish; and *C. vagabundus,* the vagabond butterflyfish. Most other species are difficult, but not impossible. Some of the most beautiful are the hardest to keep and definitely to be avoided by beginners. Do not touch *C. trifasciatus,* the melon butterflyfish; *C. meyeri,* Meyer's butterflyfish, *C. ornatissimus,* which does not seem to have a

A juvenile Threadfin Butterflyfish, *Chaetodon auriga,* has a color pattern essentially like that of the adult. Photo by Dr. Herbert R. Axelrod.

This is the size best suited for aquarium life, about 2-3 inches in length. Photo by Michael Gilroy.

119

A school of butterflyfishes, many of which are the Threadfin Butterflyfish, *Chaetodon auriga*. Also visible are some surgeonfishes and a couple of parrotfishes. Photo by Dr. Warren E. Burgess.

Chaetodon auriga in its natural habitat in the Red Sea. Red Sea Filament Butterflyfishes lack the black spot in the dorsal fin. Photo by Walter Deas.

Chaetodon auriga is one of the hardier species of butterflyfishes. It accepts a variety of foods both living and prepared. Photo by Dr. Herbert R. Axelrod.

The Filament Butterflyfish received its common name from the filamentous extension of the dorsal fin well illustrated in this photo. Photo by Walter Deas.

Chaetodon capistratus is one of the hardier species of Western Atlantic butterflyfishes. It also is not very expensive. Photo by Ken Lucas, Steinhart Aquarium.

The Four-eyed Butterflyfish in its natural habitat at Grand Bahama Island. Photo by Dr. Patrick L. Colin.

The common name refers to the large posterior spot as a false eye. The two spots and the two true eyes make it a Four-eyed Butterflyfish. Photo by Dr. Herbert R. Axelrod.

A Four-eyed Butterflyfish in the process of metamorphosing from a silvery pelagic larval stage. Photo by Dr. Warren E. Burgess.

Small juveniles actually have two posterior spots, though the upper one disappears quickly. Photo by Aaron Norman.

A slightly older individual that has already lost its upper spot. Juveniles may be caught as far north as Cape Cope in late summer or early autumn. Photo by Aaron Norman.

A photo of *Chaetodon ephippium* taken at night in its natural habitat. This individual may be asleep or just awakened. Photo by Scott Johnson.

An adult *Chaetodon ephippium*. Illustration by Arita.

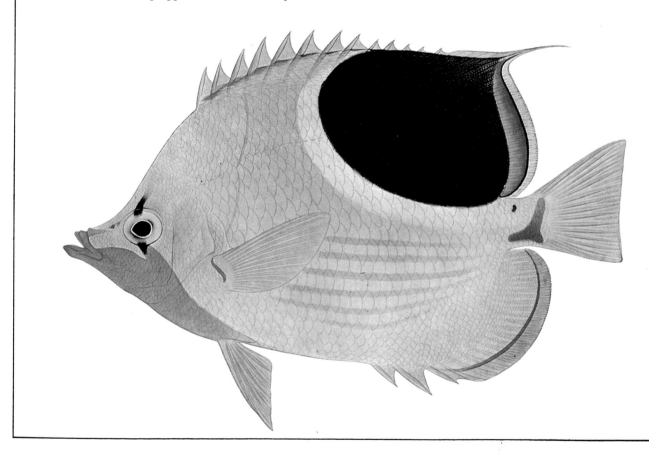

A young adult Saddle Butterflyfish, *Chaetodon ephippium*, with the dorsal filament still growing. Saddle Butterflyfish do relatively well in captivity. Photo by Allan Power.

A newly metamorphosed *Chaetodon ephippium*. The saddle is already present and will develop further. The eye band and caudal peduncle band are developed but will disappear. Photo by Dr. Fujio Yasuda.

An aggregation of *Chaetodon lunula* on a coral reef at Hawaii. Photo by Paul Allen at a depth of 50 feet.

An adult Raccoon Butterflyfish, *Chaetodon lunula*. This species is relatively hardy and does well in captivity. Photo by Ken Lucas, Steinhart Aquarium.

The juvenile Raccoon Butterflyfish has a somewhat different pattern, including a spot in the soft dorsal fin and no triangular band from the gill cover to the dorsal fin. Photo by Dr. Fujio Yasuda.

An intermediate stage with elements of both adult and juvenile *Chaetodon lunula*. Raccoon Butterflyfish are commonly available to aquarists. Photo by K. H. Choo.

Chaetodon melannotus in its natural habitat. Photo by Michio Goto, Marine Life Documents.

This tiny Black Back Butterflyfish, *Chaetodon melannotus*, appears very much like the adult. Photo by Allan Power.

A young adult Black Back Butterflyfish. The two light spots in the dusky background of the upper back are part of the fright or sleeping pattern. Photo by Dr. Herbert R. Axelrod.

A very young *Chaetodon vagabundus*. Photo by Glen S. Axelrod.

Chaetodon rafflesi in its natural habitat in the Marshall Islands. Photo by Scott Johnson.

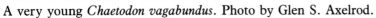

Chaetodon vagabundus is a very common butterflyfish on reefs of the Indo-Pacific. Photo by Dr. Gerald R. Allen on the Great Barrier Reef of Australia.

A cleared and stained specimen of *Chaetodon vagabundus*. This method provides more information to the scientist than a simple X-ray. Photo by Glen S. Axelrod.

Two young Raffles Butterflyfish, *Chaetodon rafflesi*. The dorsal black spot expands to form the dark fin edge of the adult. Photo by Allan Power.

Most aquarium specimens of the Vagabond Butterflyfish are about this size (2 inches). Photo by Dr. Warren E. Burgess.

An adult Raffles Butterflyfish, *Chaetodon rafflesi*. The reticulated pattern of the scales makes identification easy. Photo by Dr. Herbert R. Axelrod.

An adult *Chaetodon vagabundus* from Tahiti. This species is generally hardy and does well in marine aquaria. Photo by Dr. John E. Randall.

A juvenile Melon Butterflyfish, *Chaetodon trifasciatus*. The pattern differs from the adult as you can see. Photo by Dr. Herbert R. Axelrod.

An adult *Chaetodon trifasciatus*. This specimen was photographed by Dr. Herbert R. Axelrod in the Solomon Islands.

A Melon Butterflyfish in its natural habitat. This species is not easy to keep and should be avoided. It requires living coral. Photo by Allan Power.

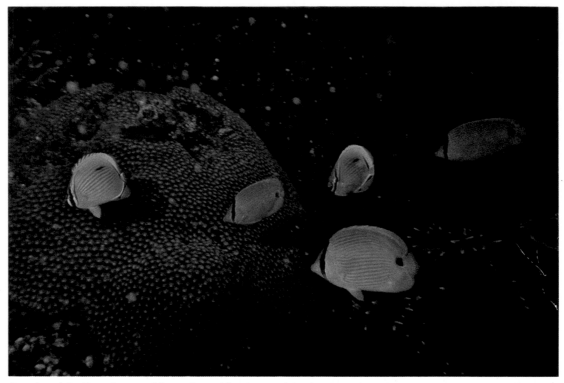

A pair of Indian Ocean *Chaetodon trifasciatus* with the orange caudal base and three *Chaetodon plebeius* on a Sri Lankan reef. Photo by Rodney Jonklaas.

The Pacific Ocean form of *Chaetodon trifasciatus* lacks the orange at the base of the caudal. Photo by Roy O'Conner.

Chaetodon meyeri is easily recognized by the pattern of black lines. Photo by Dr. Fujio Yasuda.

The juvenile Meyer's Butterflyfish has black lines but not quite the same as those of the adult. Photo by Earl Kennedy.

Chaetodon meyeri is not a common species and does poorly in captivity. It is rarely offered for sale in pet shops. Photo by Dr. Herbert R. Axelrod of a specimen captured in the Maldive Islands.

Meyer's Butterflyfish needs living coral to survive. This individual is nipping at some *Pocillopora* on a Sri Lankan reef. Photo by Rodney Jonklaas.

Chaetodon ornatissimus is related to *C. meyeri*. The patterns are similar but the stripes in *C. ornatissimus* are orange. Photo by K. H. Choo.

Like Meyer's Butterflyfish, the Ornate Butterflyfish is one of the more difficult butterflyfishes to keep. Photo by K. H. Choo.

The Ornate Butterflyfish is a coral feeder and can be seen in reef areas such as this one on occasion. Normally pairs are seen and the mate to this individual no doubt is not far away. Photo by Dr. Gerald R. Allen at Spur Reef, Great Barrier Reef of Australia.

common name, or *C. collare,* the Pakistani butterflyfish. They are all next to impossible to keep successfully, mainly because they rarely eat such foods as you are likely to be able to offer.

Relatives of the genus *Chaetodon* are also attractive fishes, some easy to keep. The genus *Heniochus* offers several, of which *H. acuminatus,* the wimple fish or poor man's Moorish idol, is the commonest, cheapest and easiest to keep. It is also probably the best looker, with black and white stripes and yellow on the dorsal and tail fins. All the members of the genus have prolonged anterior dorsals, but *H. acuminatus* has the longest fin, trailing well behind the tail in an undamaged specimen. It grows to about 10″.

Chelmon rostratus, the copper-band butterflyfish, is another attractively striped fish with, as its name suggests, coppery colored and white stripes and a long beak. Its only drawback is difficulty in feeding but the same trick as for chaetodons usually works. *Forciper flavissimus,* the long-nosed butterflyfish, has a really long beak, indicative as with *Chelmon* of a coral eater. Despite this, it is easier to feed than the copper-band and makes a good aquarium fish.

A young *Chaetodon collare*, commonly known as the Pakistani Butterflyfish and the Red-tailed Butterflyfish. Highly colorful, this species is very difficult to keep.

The adult Red-tailed Butterflyfish is still a magnificent fish. Live coral is again suggested if an attempt is made to keep it in captivity. Photo by Dr. D. Terver, Nancy Aquarium, France.

Two young Wimple Butterflyfish, also called Pennant Butterflyfish and Poor Man's Moorish Idol, *Heniochus acuminatus*. The species is considered inexpensive, colorful, and easy to keep. What more could anyone ask for?

Normally only one spine is elongate in *Heniochus*. In this *Heniochus acuminatus* two spines have become elongate. Except for a little extra drag while swimming this should not hamper the fish any. Photo by Dr. Fujio Yasuda.

These young Pennant Butterflyfish are feeding on some freeze-dried tubificid worms. Accompanying them are a couple of *Amphiprion ocellaris*. Photo by J. A. Lomas.

These two *Heniochus acuminatus* were photographed at a depth of 50 feet about a half mile off Kealoha Point, Hawaii, by Paul Allen.

In nature the streamer of the Pennant Butterflyfish's fin can grow longer than it could in captivity. This one is exceptionally long. Photo by Allan Power.

The Copperband Butterflyfish, *Chelmon rostratus*, can be kept successfully if it can be enticed to eat. This can be accomplished with patience. Photo by Burkhard Kahl.

This Copperband Butterflyfish is being cleaned by one of the cleaner shrimps, *Lysmata amboinensis*. Photo by Arend van den Nieuwenhuizen.

The Copperband Butterflyfish is a delicate feeder. The extended snout is used almost like a pair of forceps. Photo by Dr. D. Terver, Nancy Aquarium.

Chelmon rostratus, like many other butterflyfishes, has a false eye-spot in the soft dorsal fin and the true eye is masked by a band of color.

An early illustration of the Copperband Butterflyfish from the *Philippine Journal of Science*.

The snout of *Forcipiger flavissimus* is much longer than that of the Copperband Butterflyfish and can reach further into the crevices for food. Photo by Dr. Herbert R. Axelrod.

The coral reef offers *Forcipiger flavissimus* many crevices in which to hide. Photo by Walter Deas, Great Barrier Reef.

A young Long-nosed Butterflyfish, *Forcipiger flavissimus*. The antics of this species swimming around a tank through the corals and picking at morsels of food are a delight to watch. Photo by Dr. Herbert R. Axelrod.

ACANTHURIDAE

This is the family of surgeons or tangs, widely distributed around tropical seas. Characteristically rather large fishes when fully adult, around a foot or more in length, they are mostly very attractive when young, but fast growers if properly fed. Their diet must include plenty of vegetation, frozen lettuce, or spinach, if natural algae are not available. The combination of a demanding diet and fast growth when it is supplied puts them

A Blue Surgeonfish, *Paracanthurus hepatus*, in its natural habitat at Madang, New Guinea. Photo by Dr. Gerald R. Allen.

This beautiful Blue Surgeonfish is one of the easiest of surgeonfishes to keep. Photo by Burkhard Kahl.

The surgeonfish diet should include plenty of vegetable matter. Photo by Gerhard Marcuse.

The Blue Surgeonfish, *Paracanthurus hepatus*, can often be seen browsing on the algae or plants of the reef. Normally this species is seen in aggregations rather than solitary individuals. Photo by Allan Power.

Acanthurus leucosternon picking algae from the coral reef. Photo by Dr. Wolfgang Klausewitz.

It is always interesting to speculate on the significance of the various patterns and colors of the brightly colored reef fishes like this *Acanthurus leucosternon*. Photo by Dr. Herbert R. Axelrod of a specimen from the Maldive Islands.

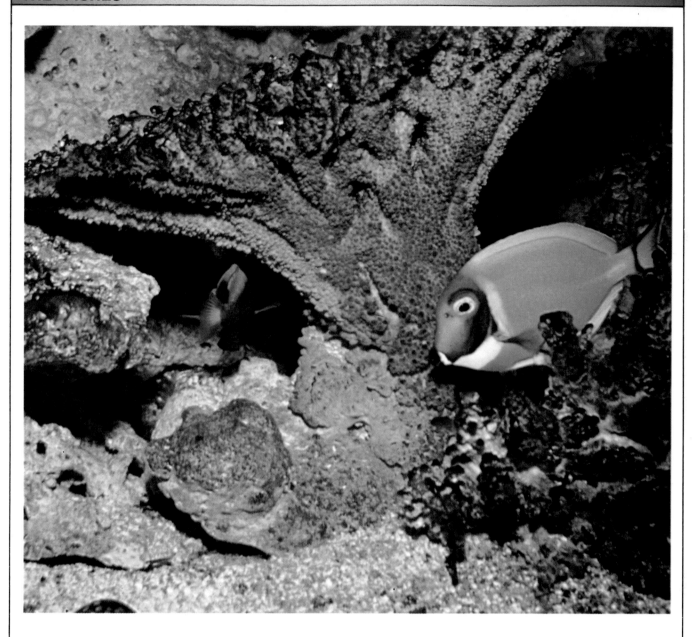

into Group 2. Also few are cheap. They need careful handling too, as they have a pair of sharp spines at the base of the tail that can cut the owner's hand.

The most popular of the surgeons is probably *Paracanthurus hepatus,* the blue surgeon, with its bright blue body and black markings. It is also one of the easiest to keep, although growing larger than is usually stated in the literature. Its rival, the powder blue tang, *Acanthurus leucosternon,* is equally attractive but expensive and touchy in comparison. Both come from the Indo-Pacific. Another beauty, *A. lineatus,* the clown surgeon, has blue stripes on a yellow body, grows quite large, but is well worth having.

The genus *Zebrasoma* has several spectacular members. *Z. xanthurum,* the purple tang, that grows up to 2 feet however; *Z. flavescens,* the yellow tang, a popular species growing only to

With surgeonfishes like this Powder Blue Tang present in a tank there should be plenty of algae available. Photo by Dr. Herbert R. Axelrod.

Compared to *Paracanthurus hepatus, Acanthurus leucosternon* is harder to keep and more expensive as well.

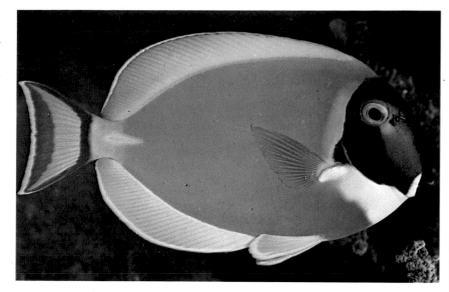

The name surgeonfish refers to the scalpel-like spine at the base of the tail. In the Powder Blue Surgeonfish it is well advertised in yellow. Photo by Burkhard Kahl.

about 7″, *Z. desjardinii,* the sailfin tang, with large striped dorsal and ventral fins, and its close relative, *Z. veliferum,* also a sailfin.

The genus *Naso,* the unicorn tangs, grow nasal protuberances as adults in most species, not seen in young specimens. The most popular member, *N. lituratus,* the smoothhead unicorn fish, doesn't have such a development, even as adult, but does have an attractive pair of long tail filaments and striking colors that change from purplish in the young to red and yellow in the adult. Some forms, however, are quite dull in color and unacceptable.

►
A Clown Surgeonfish photographed at Marau, Solomon Islands by Dr. Herbert R. Axelrod.

◄
This pretty fish is the Clown Surgeonfish, *Acanthurus lineatus.* It is always in demand by aquarists. Photo by Allan Power.

The peduncle spine is not distinctly marked in the Clown Surgeonfish. Photo by Dr. D. Terver, Nancy Aquarium, France.
►

The Yellowtail Sailfin Tang, *Zebrasoma xanthurum*, is commonly also known as the Purple Tang. Photo by Dr. D. Terver, Nancy Aquarium, France.

Diet and lighting make a big difference in the coloration of *Zebrasoma xanthurum*. Perhaps this darkish individual is frightened. Photo by Dr. Herbert R. Axelrod.

This is a young Yellowtail Sailfin Tang in its natural habitat in the Red Sea. Young *Zebrasoma* species generally have higher dorsal and anal fins than adults. The yellow tail of the common name is quite conspicuous. Photo by Norbert Shuh.

The Yellow Sailfin Tang, *Zebrasoma flavescens*, occasionally will become blotched yellow and white as seen in this individual. The reasons are not currently known. Fortunately, the fish commonly regain the overall yellow color of the species and seem no worse for wear. Photo by Dr. Herbert R. Axelrod.

This 5-inch Yellow Sailfin Tang was photographed in its natural habitat at about a depth of 30 feet a half mile off Kealoha Point, Hawaii. Photo by Paul Allen.

The Yellow Sailfin Tang, *Zebrasoma flavescens*, in its normal color. The caudal peduncle spine is not yellow but a contrasting white. Photo by Dr. D. Terver, Nancy Aquarium, France.

A juvenile Desjardin's Sailfin Tang, *Zebrasoma desjardinii*. This is the size at which aquarists generally see them for sale. Photo by Ray Allard.

An adult Desjardin's Sailfin Tang has a somewhat different color pattern. Note that the peduncle spine is also marked by color. Photo by Dr. D. Terver, Nancy Aquarium, France.

Many fishes become quite tame in their natural habitat and will accept food from divers. Sudden moves will quickly send them to the nearest refuge so a slow, patient approach is necessary. If the fishes are too wary of the divers they may be attracted by leaving some food items on the bottom and watching from a distance. Photo by Helmut Debelius in the Red Sea.

Although quite dark the pattern of this *Zebrasoma desjardinii* can still be detected. Photo by Dr. Herbert R. Axelrod of a specimen from the Maldive Islands.

The Pacific Sailfin Tang, *Zebrasoma veliferum*. These are juveniles with very high dorsal and anal fins, a characteristic of the genus. Photo by Douglas Faulkner.

This is a very small Pacific Sailfin Tang, *Zebrasoma veliferum*. The dorsal and anal fins are just starting to become elongate. After a while the body will grow proportionately faster again and the fins will appear less elongate. Photo by Aaron Norman.

The Pacific Sailfin Tang is closely related to Desjardin's Sailfin Tang but is confined to the Pacific Ocean; Desjardin's Sailfin Tang is an Indian Ocean species. Photo by Walter Deas on the Great Barrier Reef of Australia.

The Cleaner Wrasse *Labroides dimidiatus* is examining this Orange-spine Unicornfish, *Naso lituratus*, for parasites. Photo by Gunter Spies.

The Orange-spine or Smoothhead Unicornfish, *Naso lituratus*, develops long filaments on the caudal fin but lacks the frontal protuberance of some other members of the genus. Photo by Dr. Herbert R. Axelrod.

A juvenile *Naso lituratus* from Hawaii. The dorsal and anal fins already have the color of the adults. Photo by Dr. Herbert R. Axelrod.

Drawing of an adult *Naso lituratus*, called both the Smoothhead Unicornfish and the Orange-spine Unicornfish. At this stage in the fish's development the tail filaments are present.

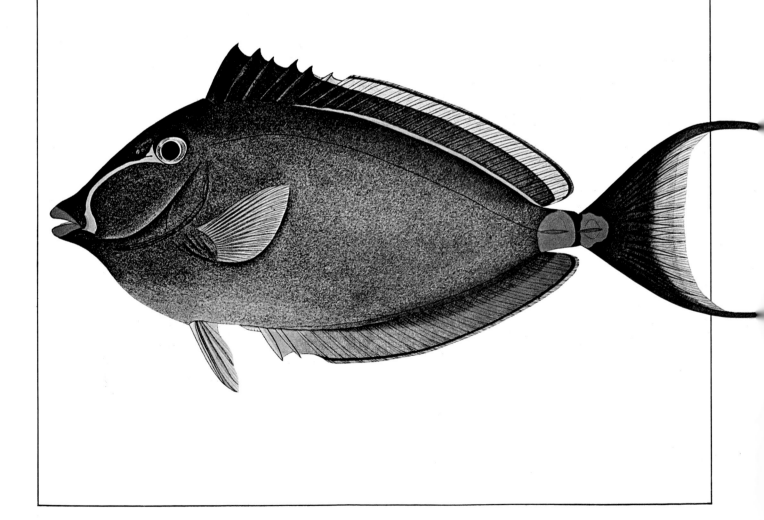

The Orange-spine Unicornfish has a pair of sharp, immovable spines on the caudal peduncle. They are advertised by the bright orange color. Photo by Dr. Herbert R. Axelrod.

EPHIPPIDAE

Even worse than the surgeons, the batfishes grow big and grow fast. When young they are all most attractive, but tend to lose some of their beauty as they rapidly grow, unless you restrict their diet. There are three species commonly available, but none should be purchased unless you have a large, deep tank or are prepared to dispose of them when they grow too big. *Platax orbicularis*, the orbiculate

The tank housing the Orbiculate Batfish, *Platax orbicularis*, should be large as it is easy to keep and grows quite large in a very short period of time. Photo by Douglas Faulkner.

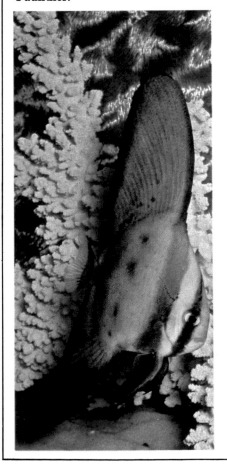

Young Orbiculate Batfish resemble dead leaves that fall into the water along mangrove lined shores and are hard to detect. Photo by Dr. Shih-Chieh Shen.

The adult Orbiculate Batfish is less attractiive than the juvenile. This subadult is being cleaned by a *Labroides dimidiatus*. Photo by Dr. Herbert R. Axelrod.

batfish, grows to about 20″ and is deeper than it is long, with very fully developed dorsal and anal fins. It becomes very tame and quite a pet. It is found almost anywhere tropical except the Atlantic. *P. teira,* the round-faced batfish from the Indo-Pacific, is a beauty when young and can be three or four times as tall as it is long, but as usual grows like a mushroom and can get to 2 feet in length. *P. pinnatus,* the long-finned bat fish, is the gem of the collection. High-priced, rather delicate and difficult to feed sometimes, it is not for beginners. When young it is almost black bodied with red margins all round, that regrettably fade as growth proceeds. A most spectacular fish. Why are the best-looking usually the touchiest?

A fully adult *Platax orbicularis* is quite a large fish and only suitable for display tanks or public aquariums. This individual was photographed at a depth of 30 feet at the Great Barrier Reef of Australia by Walter Deas.

Two *Labroides dimidiatus* are working together to clean parasites from the gills of this adult Orbiculate Batfish. Photo by Walter Deas on the Great Barrier Reef.

Platax pinnatus is the most spectacular batfish but it is also the most difficult to keep. Photo by Burkhard Kahl.

An intermediate-sized *Platax pinnatus* in its natural habitat in the Solomon Islands. Some remnants of the color of the juvenile still remain. Photo by Wade Doak.

Small groups of batfish can often be seen on the reef. Here several *Platax pinnatus* adults (15 to 18 inches in length) are feeding at Euston Reef, Great Barrier Reef, Australia. Photo by Dr. Gerald R. Allen.

A Round-faced Batfish, *Platax teira*, submitting to the cleaning procedures of *Labroides dimidiatus*. Photo by Walter Deas at Heron Island, Great Barrier Reef.

Young *Platax teira* are intermediate in appeal to aquarists. They are also intermediate in hardiness, being more delicate than *P. orbicularis* but hardier than *P. pinnatus*. Photo by Klaus Paysan.

When batfishes get to be this big (about half-grown) the aquarium housing it should be upwards of 100-gallon capacity. The long dorsal and anal fins also dictate that the tank be deep as well. Photo by Walter Deas.

Some cover is necessary for the batfishes. Behind this *Platax teira* can be seen bleached corals that are commonly used for aquarium decorations. Photo by Dr. Fujio Yasuda.

A subadult *Platax teira* with its elongate fins still evident. Photo by Walter Deas. ▲

BALISTIDAE (MONACANTHINAE)

The filefishes are mainly polyp feeders, but can be weaned with some difficulty in the aquarium onto brine shrimp or other live food and eventually even frozen or flake foods. They are also relatives of the triggerfishes, but quite peaceful and grow only to a few inches in length.

The long-nosed filefish, *Oxymonacanthus longirostris,* from the Indo-Pacific, is the most frequently offered and is quite a striking fish, with yellow spots and blotches on a green background. The fantailed filefish, *Pervagor spilosoma,* is almost as attractive. It has a blue and yellow body with black dots and markings and a red

The Long-nosed Filefish, *Oxymonacanthus longirostris*, is one of the most frequently offered of the filefishes. Photo by Dr. Herbert R. Axelrod. ▼

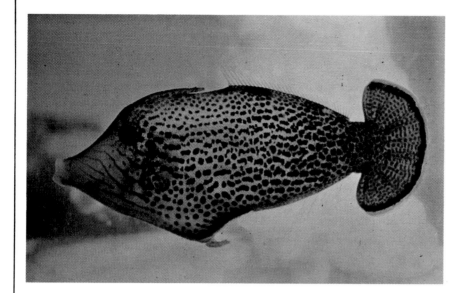

The Fantailed Filefish, *Pervagor spilosoma*, with its colorful tail fully spread. Photo by Dr. Herbert R. Axelrod.

Pervagor spilosoma at a depth of 30 feet off Kahe Point, Oahu. Photo by Dr. Gerald R. Allen.

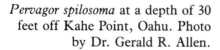

Try catching this *Oxymonacanthus longirostris* in this stand of *Acropora* coral. Photo by Michio Goto, *Marine Life Documents*.

179

tail. *Cantherhines pullus,* the tail-light filefish, is hardy and cheap, coming from the Atlantic, and is a vegetarian. Its quite beautiful relative, *C. macroceros,* also from the Atlantic, is, unfortunately, rare and expensive.

The Tail-light Filefish, *Cantherhines pullus.* This individual was collected at St. John, Virgin Islands. Photo by Dr. John E. Randall.

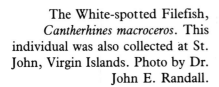

The White-spotted Filefish, *Cantherhines macroceros.* This individual was also collected at St. John, Virgin Islands. Photo by Dr. John E. Randall.

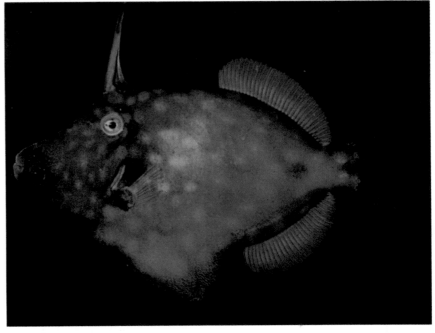

The white "tail light" of this *Cantherhines pullus* is quite distinct. Photo by Dr. Dwayne Reed at San Salvador.

A young *Cantherhines macroceros* searching for food on an algal flat off Margarita Reef, Puerto Rico. Photo by Charles Arneson. ►

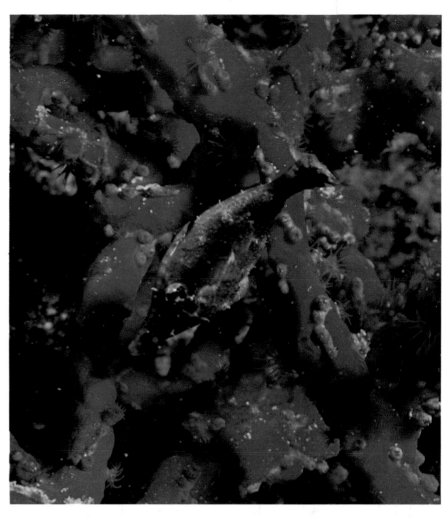

An adult *Cantherhines macroceros* in its natural habitat off the island of Bonaire. Photo by Dr. Dwayne Reed. ▼

▲
The Lyretail Coralfish, *Anthias squamipinnis*, is commonly available to aquarists. It does best in small groups. Photo by Dr. Herbert R. Axelrod.

SERRANIDAE (ANTHIINAE)

Sea-perches are small to moderate-sized coral or deeper-sea fishes, becoming popular because of their splendid colors. *Anthias squamipinnis,* the lyretail coral fish, is perhaps the best known, but there are many different species from the Indo-Pacific. *Mirolabrichthys tuka,* the purple queen, is a related fish, but hard to keep.

▲ A few Lyretail Coralfish hovering over part of a coral reef. Sometimes several hundred of these fishes may be seen on one small patch of reef. Photo by Helmut Debelius in the Red Sea.

◄
Small groupers, like this *Anthias squamipinnis*, do well in captivity. The upper fish is "yawning" a common behavior in fishes. Photo by Michio Goto, *Marine Life Documents*.

These young Purple Queens are dangerously close to the open jaws of a Blackcheek Moray Eel. Photo by Dr. Dwayne Reed.

The Purple Queen, *Mirolabrichthys tuka*, is hard to keep. Photo of a specimen captured at Marau, Solomon Islands, by Dr. Herbert R. Axelrod.

A group of Purple Queens in their natural habitat on a coral reef. A large male can be seen about in the center of the photo. Photo by Wade Doak.

GROUP 3

Now we come to the fishes to avoid, some because they are very hard to keep, some because they are vicious, get too big quickly, or are, frankly, predators. Many are very nice fishes, perfectly easy to keep if on their own or with equally large and tough tank mates, but it is assumed that you don't want a small collection of big fishes or only one species in your aquarium at this stage. If you do, there are fishes to select from here. I have already mentioned a few of the no-nos—*Pygoplites diacanthus* and some of the chaetodons, for example, that just will not feed nine times out of ten, or worse.

The Polka Dot Grouper, *Cromileptes altivelis*, is fine for aquaria when small but it grows to a length of two feet. Photo by Burkhard Kahl.

This Polka Dot Grouper is about a foot in length already but it still retains some of its color. Photo by Dr. D. Terver, Nancy Aquarium, France.

SERRANIDAE (SERRANINAE)

The groupers include some beautiful fishes, but they are predators and will snap up any small fishes available. They may be kept with other equally large fishes, but realize that they grow fast. In captivity, they will eat any meaty fish foods. Perhaps the commonest of the Indo-Pacific groupers is *Cromileptes altivelis,* the polka dot grouper, that grows to be a fine table fish and quite expensive to eat. It gets to about 2 feet in length. *Mycteroperca venenosa* the yellowfin grouper, is fit only for a public aquarium, growing to 3 feet in length and like most groupers, becoming very tame. A pity that such handsome fishes have a serious drawback.

Grammistes sexlineatus, the golden striped grouper is another beauty that doesn't grow quite so big, but has a voracious appetite for any smaller fishes. It is placed in the family Grammistidae.

The Golden-striped Grouper, *Grammistes sexlineatus*, is quite attractive but could also be quite deadly. In addition to its large appetite it also exudes a poisonous slime when frightened. Photo by Dr. Gerald R. Allen at Palau.

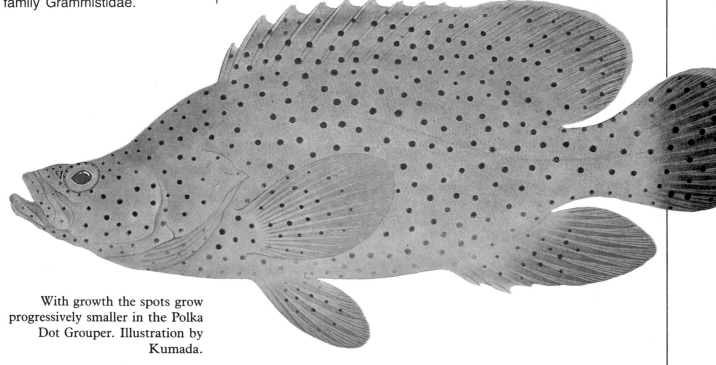

With growth the spots grow progressively smaller in the Polka Dot Grouper. Illustration by Kumada.

The pattern of the Golden-striped or Six-lined Grouper is quite striking and sorely tempts aquarists who see it for sale. Photo by Dr. Fujio Yasuda.

Golden-striped Groupers also attain a fairly large size (about a foot or so) and look best as juveniles. Photo by Gene Wolfsheimer.

BALISTIDAE (BALISTINAE)

The triggerfishes have already been discussed, and it is sufficient to state that most grow large and offensive. Particular mention must be reserved for *Balistoides conspicillum* the clown triggerfish, one of the most striking fishes available, with its blue or white spotted belly and yellow and orange dorsal markings. It is possible to come across a fairly well behaved, usually small clown trigger, but never bet on it! Most specimens are vicious and attack not only

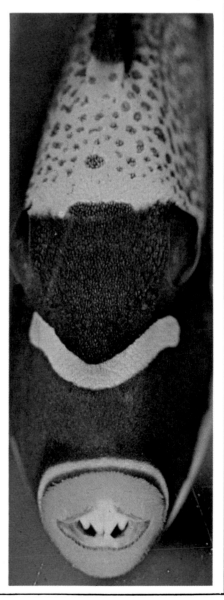

A Clown Triggerfish, *Balistoides conspicillum*, in its natural habitat. This adult was photographed at Euston Reef, Great Barrier Reef, Australia at a depth of about 30 feet. Photo by Dr. Gerald R. Allen.

◄
The teeth of balistids, for example this Clown Triggerfish, are strong and can do much damage to equipment as well as other fishes. Photo by Dr. Shih-Chieh Shen.

other fishes, but their owner, airlines, cables, and anything else available. Some end a life of crime by electrocuting themselves, a fitting but expensive finish.

SCORPAENIDAE

The lionfishes, also known as turkeyfishes, butterfly cod, and dragonfishes, owe their names to their spreading pectoral and dorsal fins. They are all predatory, but will learn to take dead meat or fish if gradually weaned to it. They are not aggressive and are quite safe with anything they cannot swallow, which means fishes as large or nearly as large as themselves. Most of the popular species belong to the genus *Pterois,* the most famous being

Juvenile Clown Triggerfish may be acceptable in a community tank for a while but may become very aggressive as they grow . Photo by Dr. Herbert R. Axelrod.

It is hard to resist a fish so beautiful but its initial cost and the prospect of its doing much damage should deter most marine enthusiasts. Photo by K. H. Choo.

The lionfishes, like this *Pter ois volitans*, are among the favorite aquarium fishes — but they can be deadly. The long feather-like fin spines are provided with poison sacs. Photo by Allan Power.

A juvenile Lionfish, *Pterois volitans*, and a Spotted Hawkfish at Byron Bay, New South Wales. Photo by Walter Deas.

Two striking lionfishes. The upper fish is *Pterois volitans*, the lower fish *Pterois antennata*. Both are venomous.

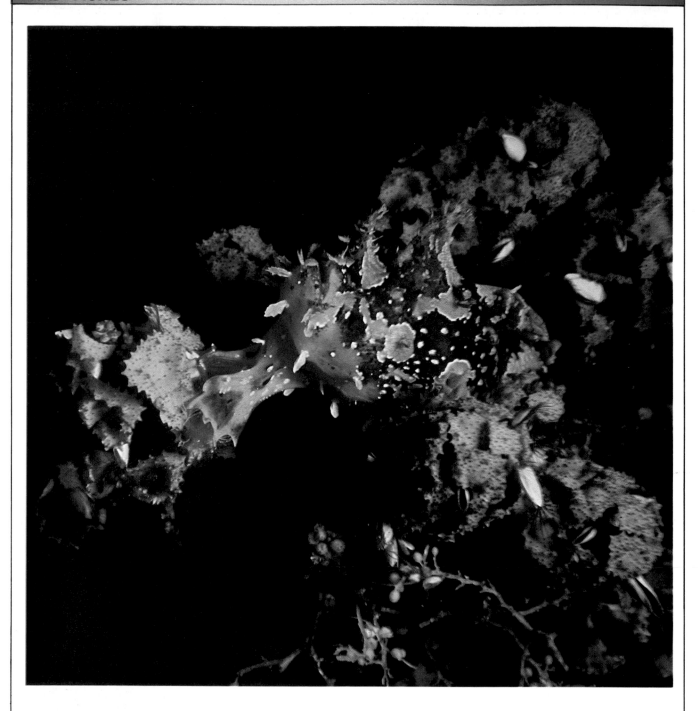

P. volitans. All have poison spines on the dorsal fin and must be handled with care. A large specimen can kill a human! They come from the Pacific and Indian Oceans and the Red Sea.

ANTENNARIIDAE

Another Indo-Pacific family contains the anglerfishes, with one well-known species, *Histrio histrio,* the sargassum fish, extending to the tropical Atlantic as well. They are all predators, with some temperate-sea cousins that are large, ugly, and unattractive and some deep-sea cousins that are positively hideous. The same goes for them as for the lionfishes. They are not aggressive but will

The Sargassumfish, *Histrio histrio*, is a camouflage expert, blending almost completely into the Sargassum Weed in which it lives. Photo by Neville Coleman.

With the Sargassum removed *Histrio histrio* can be seen more clearly. Photo by Dr. Herbert R. Axelrod.

The Sargassumfish is notorious for being able to swallow fishes almost as big as they are. They eat their own kind as well.

swallow anything small enough, which means nearly as big as they are. They can be taught to eat dead food, but then they lose their interesting habit of "angling" with the modified spine on the nose. This carries a bait, often capable of wriggling actively to attract prey.

ZANCLIDAE

This family has only one member, *Zanclus canescens,* the Moorish Idol. Many of us go on trying to keep this fish, usually with no success, as it just will not eat. It is a harmless, beautiful fish, subject to disease very easily and certainly not for beginners.

The Moorish Idol, *Zanclus canescens,* is just as delicate as it is beautiful. Photo by Michio Goto, *Marine Life Documents.*

A night photo of the Moorish Idol in its natural habitat. It is relatively easy to collect this fish at night. Photo by Michio Goto, *Marine Life Documents.*

In rather drab surroundings the Moorish Idol sticks out like the proverbial sore thumb. This individual was photographed in the Maldive Islands by Dr. Herbert R. Axelrod.

▲
The Moorish Idol has a range extending across the entire Indo-Pacific as far as the coast of Mexico. The butterflyfish is *Pseudochaetodon nigrirostris*. Photo by Alex Kerstitch at Cabo San Lucas.

►
The Moorish Idol has been used in aquatic design for many years. Photo by Dr. Herbert R. Axelrod.

SYNGNATHIDAE

This is the family of seahorses and pipefishes. The genus *Hippocampus* is very widely distributed in both temperate and tropical seas, and contains the sea horses. The tropical species are sometimes spectacular. The pipefishes fall into a variety of genera and are more restricted to the tropics. All feed exclusively on live foods and will in general not learn to take anything else. Success with seahorses has been claimed with frozen *Mysis* shrimps however. It is cruel to try to keep these fishes unless a supply of acceptable food can be guaranteed. Furthermore, it is equally cruel to keep them with ordinary fishes that will snap up any live food before the slow- feeding seahorses or pipefishes can get at it.

One of the common Indo-Pacific sea horses is *Hippocampus kuda*. Photo by Burkhard Kahl.

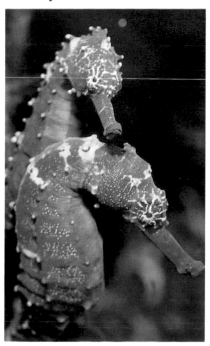

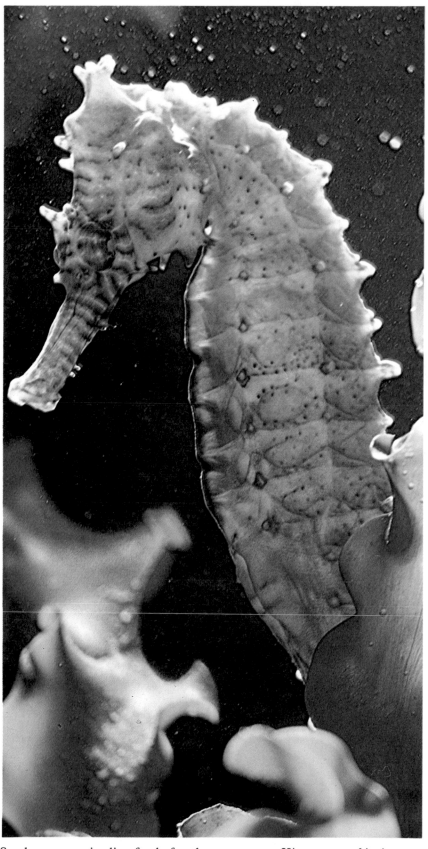

Sea horses require live foods for the most part. *Hippocampus histrix* seen here is using some marine algae as a holdfast.

Some sea horses are quite spectacular. These *Hippocampus bargibanti* from the New Hebrides are well camouflaged on this sea fan. Photo by Allan Power.

The Knobby Sea Horse, *Hippocampus breviceps*, is another attractive species. It may be worth one's while to provide live foods to such species to keep them alive. Photo by Dr. Gerald R. Allen. ►

The Weedy Sea Dragon, *Phyllopteryx taeniolatus*, is found in Australian waters. This would make some addition to a marine aquarium. Photo by Dr. Gerald R. Allen. ◄

Young Weedy Sea Dragons are not as colorful as the adults and can blend into the weeds better. Photo by Dr. Gerald R. Allen.

The Leafy Sea Dragon, *Phycodorus eques*, is also quite striking. Like sea horses they require live foods and a quiet tank. Photo by Dr. Gerald R. Allen.

CALLIONYMIDAE

The same as for the Syngnathidae can be said of this family, the dragonets. It has some very attractive, small members, outstandingly *Pterosynchiropus splendidus,* the Mandarin fish and *Synchiropus picturatus,* the green-ringed dragonet. They are slow feeders on live food of all types and tend gradually to starve if not properly cared for.

Synchiropus picturatus is also a slow feeder on live foods. This species should be reserved for advanced hobbyists. Photo by Burkhard Kahl.

Synchiropus picturatus is also called the Psychodelic Dragonet because of its bizarre pattern. Photo by Dr. Herbert R. Axelrod.

A head-on view of the Mandarin Dragonet, *Pterosynchiropus splendidus*. The mouth is very small but can handle even adult brine shrimp. Photo by Dr. Herbert R. Axelrod.

Pterosynchiropus splendidus roams all over the scenery feeding on small prey and mates high up in the water. Its eggs and young are planktonic. Photo by Dr. Herbert R. Axelrod.

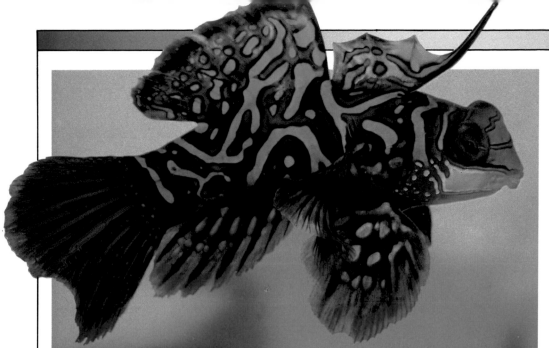

Pterosynchiropus splendidus is certainly a splendidly colored species. Why should such beauties be so difficult to keep? Photo by Burkhard Kahl.

The Mandarin Dragonet is very goby-like but is in an entirely different family. Photos by Burkhard Kahl.

Invertebrates

In a freshwater aquarium lies the opportunity to keep rather few invertebrates, an enormous contrast to the marine tank. There is a whole world of fascinating creatures not found elsewhere and it seems a great pity not to take advantage of it. Yet there are complications, making it easier to restrict a tank to fishes or to invertebrates rather than to mix the majority of them together. The biggest drawback to a mixture is the treatment of fish diseases, since many remedies are liable to kill invertebrates or to affect them badly. This is true of the most frequently used medication, copper, which is lethal to crustaceans and many others. So perhaps it is wise to start, at least, with one or the other in any one aquarium and later to try mixing them, or to restrict yourself to such invertebrates as can be readily removed from a fish tank if necessary.

Fishes all belong to a single class, Pisces, of the phylum Chordata. A phylum is a group of animals all built on the same basic plan. In the case of the Chordata, which includes all vertebrate animals from lampreys to man, all have a notochord, a stiffening rod that in most develops into the backbone. In contrast, there are many invertebrate phyla, a few of which are dealt with below. Some phyla have complicated life histories that I shall only touch upon. In some instances, the young, as with caterpillars, go through several stages before becoming adult.

COELENTERATA

This phylum is characterized by radial symmetry, a single opening into the body cavity, and the production of nematocysts, stinging cells that eject poisonous barbs when touched and are both defensive and for catching prey. Its main aquarium representatives are the anemones and corals, flower-like animals with rings of tentacles surrounding the mouth and furnished with nematocysts. An anemone in association with anemonefishes is a fine sight and one of the earliest combinations you are likely to try out, but there are many smaller anemones worth keeping for their own beauty.

The anemonefishes associate with the stichodactyline anemones - the large tropical ones found on reefs and elsewhere, some even on sandy beaches below low tide. They have masses of tentacles, fairly long in some forms such as *Radianthus,* tiny in others such as *Stoichactis* or *Discosoma,* giving the appearance of terry towelling. Choose specimens of a suitable size. About 8" - 12" across would fit a 2 ft to 3 ft tank and be large enough to house the fishes. *Stoichactis* in particular can reach many feet across. (Note that I refer to genera, not to individual species of anemone). All of these large anemones need good light or they fade away, first losing color and then gradually shrinking, even if fed. This is because they lose the indwelling algae in their tissues that help to keep them alive. This is true of many other anemones as well.

There are two genera of anemones to avoid. *Cerianthus* anemones, tube anemones that burrow into the sand and extend long pastel-colored tentacles, are very attractive but sting quite badly and are likely to kill or injure other invertebrates or even fishes. The fire anemone, *Actinodendron,* is even worse and can sting its owner severely beside being dangerous to other tankmates. It looks somewhat like a tree, with branching arms and masses of small tentacles and grows to about 18" across. It also is pastel-colored, creamy or slatey usually.

Corals are anemones that secrete some sort of skeleton, soft or hard, and are usually connected up with one another in a colony of so-called polyps. There are solitary forms as well. The best-known corals are those secreting hard, limey skeletons, often used for decoration after the animals are dead. Like many of the anemones, corals typically have algae in their cells that supply much of their nourishment, while the algae live on the waste products of the coral and those in the surrounding water. Without strong light these corals die and that is their usual fate in the aquarium not adapted to their needs. Some corals, especially the "soft" corals that secrete only scattered spicules of lime in their tissues, do not have indwelling algae and so

Of all the marine invertebrates, the largest sea anemones are the most likely to be found in a tank. Because they are the natural homes of the anemonefishes, the stichodactyline anemones, such as these *Radianthus*, are considered by many hobbyists to be essential in any tank with anemonefishes. Photos by U. E. Friese.

Close up of an anemonefish nestling within the tentacles of its host anemone. Photo by David Axelrod.

Although they are sessile, many anemones are active feeders in the aquarium, but the food has to come to them. The safest way to feed is to actually put a small piece of food directly into the anemone's mouth. Art by J. R. Quinn.

Things are not always what they seem at first glance. This is a solitary coral, probably *Fungia*, not an anemone! Photo by Dr. Herbert R. Axelrod.

Next to the species of *Radianthus*, the most common large anemones are the *Stoichactis* species. These have shorter tentacles than most *Radianthus* but otherwise are not significantly different. Other animals, such as the porcelain crab, *Petrolisthes maculatus*, at the right, also make their homes in large anemones. Photo by U. E. Friese.

The "leather coral," probably *Actinodiscus* sp., is a corallimorph anemone, not a true coral or real anemone. Photo by Dr. Herbert R. Axelrod.

Stenopus hispidus, the banded coral shrimp. Photo by Dr. Herbert R. Axelrod.

can get along in moderate light. However, nearly all corals do well only in clean water and do not tolerate high nitrate concentrations, so all in all they are best avoided until the aquarist is ready to cater to their special requirements. They are predominantly filter feeders, sifting such planktonic food as they need from the water and passing it into the mouth rather than ingesting large prey, but some do the latter as well.

ARTHROPODA

This phylum includes all the animals with external skeletons and jointed legs—the insects, crustaceans, spiders, ticks, etc. It is with the crustaceans that we are concerned. As there are 25 - 30,000 species of them, we have to be very selective! It is a surprise to many that barnacles are crustaceans that have settled down after a free larval stage to become attached by the head to a surface of some kind where the creature forms its hard external plates and fishes for plankton with its feet. They do not form good aquarium subjects as they are hard to keep alive and readily pollute the tank.

The pearly white antennae of the banded coral shrimp stand out in the dark reef. Photo by B. Kahl.

Facing page: Its bright colors of red, white, and mother of pearl have made the banded coral shrimp one of the most popular marine invertebrates. Although unmated specimens will fight viciously, they seldom attack other animals in the tank. There has been some limited success in captive breeding this beautiful shrimp.

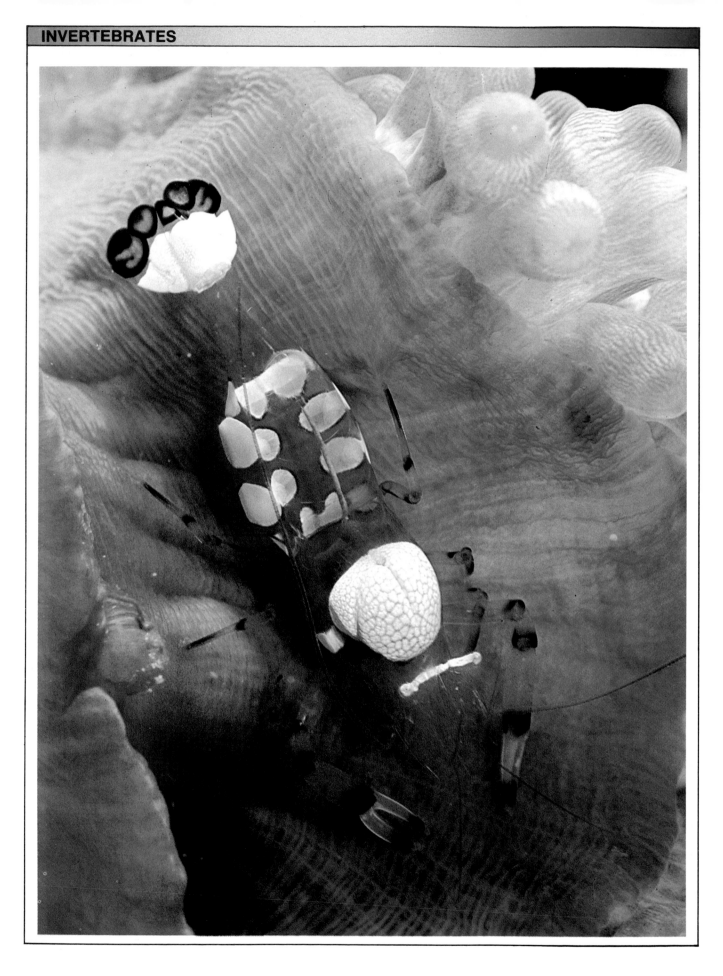

The numerous species of *Periclimenes* include a few that are suitable for the aquarium. Most are too small, too rare, or too colorless to be of interest even if they do have fascinating habits. *P. brevicarpalis* (above and facing page) is one of the largest and most heavily colored species and adapts well to the aquarium. The male is much smaller and less colorful than the female, more like the *P. lucasi* at the right. Photos of *P. brevicarpalis* by K. H. Choo, that of *P. lucasi* by A. Kerstitch.

Known by such names as the candy cane shrimp and scarlet lady, the cleaning shrimp *Lysmata grabhami* is one of the most familiar and readily available aquarium crustaceans. Few other animals can equal its brilliant vermilion, yellow, and mother of pearl color pattern. It is an active cleaner in aquaria, safely mounting fishes such as the *Chelmon rostratus* shown above and on the facing page.

Other species of *Lysmata* are occasionally available. Most, such as the *L. californica* at the upper left, are not especially attractive and some have the reputation of being unreliable microcarnivores. Others, such as the incredible *L. debelius* at the middle and below, are rare but highly desirable and quite expensive for small, often short-lived animals. Few of the small shrimps are well-known, and even fewer are bred with any success in the aquarium. Photo at top by A. Kerstitch, at middle by B. Kahl, and at bottom courtesy Dr. D. Terver, Nancy Aquarium.

Shrimps or crabs are likely to be the first to attract your attention in the pet shop. Outstanding is the readily available *Stenopus hispidus,* the banded coral shrimp. It is a cleaner, like the cleaner wrasse, but not as good at the job. It grows to about 3″ in length and has the appearance of a red and white scorpion, with its two large claws always extended - as long as it has them, for it readily sheds one or both. If this happens, don't worry, it will regrow them in subsequent moults. One day, you will think you have two shrimps instead of the one you bought, because the animal sheds a complete skeleton of itself every few weeks and grows a little larger each time. Do not buy more than one unless they are a mated pair, others always fight.

There are other attractive shrimps, some are cleaners, some live on anemones, some burrow in the substrate. See if you can obtain specimens of *Periclimenes,* a genus of pretty anemone shrimps, or of *Lysmata grabhami,* a cleaner with a redstriped back. These shrimps can be kept in any number. Avoid any of the mantis shrimps, *Squilla* and other genera, because they are predatory and furnished with knife-like appendages that can slice your hand very nastily. Avoid also the genus *Hymenocerus,* the harlequin shrimps. They are very attractive but feed on the tube feet of starfishes and are hard to accustom to any other diet. A shrimp that may give you heart failure because it produces a noise like cracking aquarium glass is the snapping shrimp, of various tropical genera.

Arrow crabs, *Stenorhynchus*. Photo below by A. Kerstitch.

Although difficult to adapt to the aquarium, the harlequin shrimps (*Hymenocerus*) are colorful and always popular. Their preferred food is the tube feet of starfishes and sometimes sea urchins, but some adapt to other foods. There are two color forms, a brown and bluish type called *elegans* from the Indian Ocean and Red Sea (shown here) and a cherry red type called *picta* from the Hawaiian Islands and probably the rest of the Pacific. These probably are not valid species, as there are intermediates, such as the one shown below. Photo at top by Dr. Herbert R. Axelrod, that below by K. H. Choo.

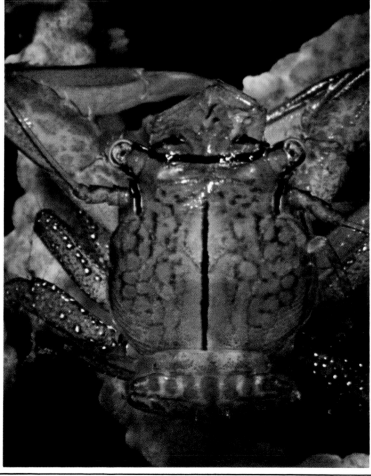

Most of the porcelain crabs, *Porcellana* and related genera, are commensals. That is, they spend most of their lives on other animals and depend on these animals for food and shelter, although they are not parasites and do not harm the host. They are found often on anemones and soft corals and survive well in the aquarium. Most are small and not especially colorful. Above is *Porcellana* sp., at right *P. furcillata*. Photos by Dr. L. P. Zann.

Sometimes one grows up undetected in the aquarium until it starts its tricks.

The usual crabs on offer are various species of hermits, inhabiting the shells of dead mollusks, occasionally covered by anemones, that the crab carefully transfers from one shell to another as it moves house. Large hermit crabs can be a nuisance, as indeed can any large crab, shifting the scenery around and picking at other precious invertebrates. Choose ones therefore that are quite small and provide them with some suitably sized shells with which to experiment. They are good scavengers and will help to keep the tank clean. Crabs proper need careful selection, large ones are dangerous and may even prey on fishes, small ones tend to hide away and might as well not be there. The arrow crab, *Stenorynchus seticornis,* is often on offer, and is a small "spider" crab, with orange or red stripes and a peaceful nature. There are many similar spider crabs of presumably similar habits. The porcelain crab, *Porcellana,* hides away, but others live on anemones and can usually be seen crawling among the tentacles.

Young stages of various lobsters are often attractively colored and tempt the aquarist, but be ready to get rid of them as they grow, which they do quite rapidly. They also have an annoying habit of stealing food from anemones, to whose stings they are immune, even fishing right down into the animal to retrieve something it has ingested. It is interesting to keep a series of moults from a crab or lobster to record its growth - one lobster I had grew from 1¼" (excluding the antennae) to 7" in just over a year, when it was given away.

Above: *Porcellana* sp., a relatively attractive porcelain crab. Although true crabs, the abdomens of the porcelain crabs are large and not held tightly under the carapace. For this reason they are often called "half crabs." Photo by Dr. L. P. Zann.

Facing page, top: Although you take a risk when you put a small lobster in the aquarium, their colors and interesting behavior often make the risk worthwhile. Few animals can surpass the brilliant colors and pattern of *Enoplometopus debelius*, the polka-dot reef lobster. Photo by A. Kerstitch.

Facing page, bottom: Slipper lobsters are less predacious than reef lobsters, but their activities constantly churn the bottom and rearrange the decorations. The Hawaiian imperial lobster, *Arctides regalis*, is sometimes available and is perhaps the most colorful of the lot. Photo by A. Norman.

ANNELIDA

There are about ten phyla of worms of one kind or another, but although many may be present in the aquarium uninvited, we are really interested in few. The annelids, segmented worms, are the most important and include the tube and featherduster worms. The most familiar to all are the earthworms and leeches, also to aquarists, tubificid worms.

The polychaete worms have conspicuous scales or bristles on each segment and are extremely common, varying in size from minute to several feet long. The free-moving forms are not of great interest, but the tube builders, with reduced bristles, offer attractive aquarium species. The serpulids build limey tubes from which they extend a crown of tentacles with many branches, hence the names fan or featherduster worms. The genus *Serpula* is colorful and large, with crowns up to 4″ across, banded with red, brown, blue, or white stripes. The sabellids build leathery tubes and offer many colorful genera, also called fan or featherduster worms. A popular genus, *Spirographis,* has corkscrew crowns up to 2″ across and very pretty, and is usually found in batches on old coral. It may be almost any color. All of these tube worms retract very quickly when disturbed, even by a shadow falling across them, but persistent predators like mandarin fishes will eventually get at least some of them. They are easy to maintain if fed fine materials up to newly hatched brine shrimp in size and will learn to accept fine powdered suspensions or "invertebrate

The only worms the aquarist is likely to purposely keep in the tank are the featherdusters and those in living rock. These large and often beautiful worms have complex crowns of fine filaments that serve as gills and also as traps for the detritus and other small foods that are eaten. Living rock (facing page) often contains many serpulids in their tubes. The only bad aspect of worms is feeding: they require very fine food suspensions that are best delivered individually to each worm (above). Art by J. R. Quinn.

The giant corkscrew featherduster, *Spirobranchus giganteus*, is probably the most attractive and sensational of the worms kept in aquaria (above and left). The gill filaments are arranged like a spiral staircase on two arms that project from a tube. The arms can be retracted and the tube closed with an ornamented operculum. Photo above by Dr. L. P. Zann, that at left by Dr. P. Colin.

Facing page: Living rock forms the basis for the mini-reef system, the numerous invertebrates (including especially the worms) serving as microfilters of detritus and conditioning the water. Photo by Dr. Herbert R. Axelrod.

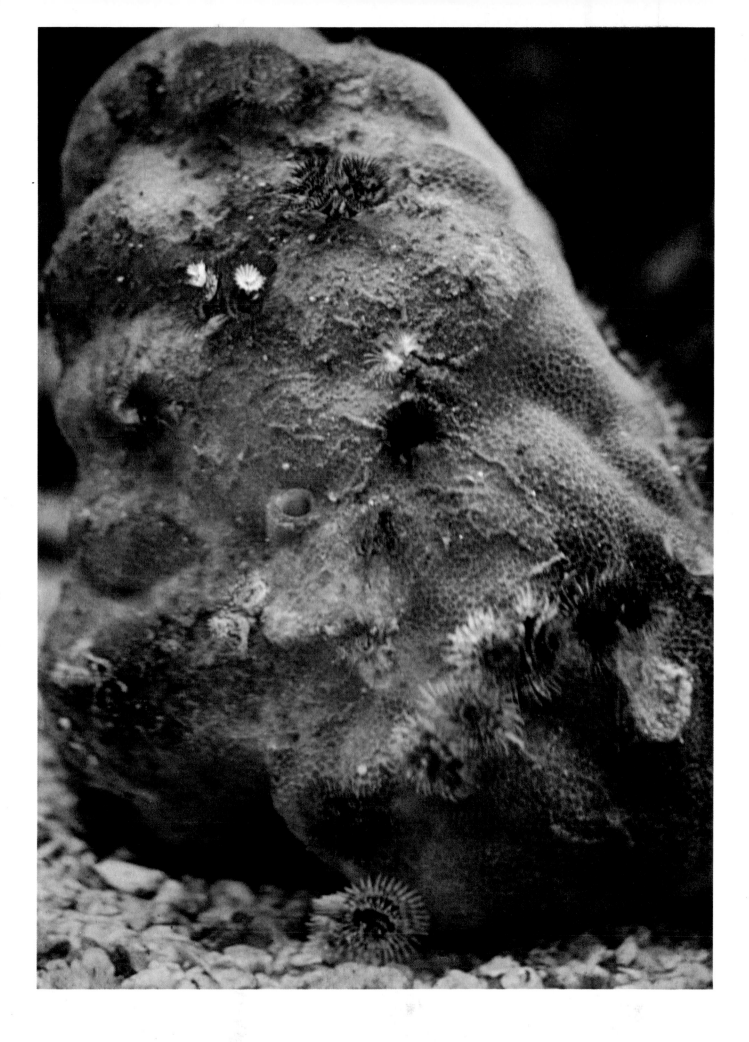

Underside of the large brittlestar *Ophiarachna incrassata*. Photo by J. Mougin, courtesy Dr. D. Terver, Nancy Aquarium, France.

food." In an invertebrate tank, they often "appear from nowhere" and may populate the tank under favorable circumstances.

ECHINODERMATA

This phylum has more creatures of interest to aquarists than possibly any other of the invertebrates. It is confined to the sea and like the coelenterates has radial symmetry, often in multiples of five. A starfish has at least five arms when intact; a sea urchin five segments to its body. Only echinoderms have tube feet, hydraulically controlled, by which they move around and adhere to surfaces, and many have spines that also aid locomotion.

The starfishes are the most popular class of echinoderms and come in a great variety of shapes and colors. Many, however, are predatory and feed in nature on bivalve mollusks by preference but on a variety of flesh if necessary. Some are filter feeders or feed on debris in the aquarium. The method used by the predators to open a clam or other bivalve is to affix themselves by their tube feet to the two halves of the shell and then to pull steadily until the prey tires and starts to open. Then the stomach is inserted into the shell and digestive juices poured in—quite a technique!

The crown of thorns starfish, *Acanthaster planci,* is a large very thorny animal that feeds on coral polyps and has recently been found in plague proportions on many Pacific reefs.

The brittle stars are so-called because most species readily

The bright green brittlestar *Ophiarachna incrassata* is fairly typical of its group except that it is larger and more colorful. It is moderately active under low light conditions and not a dangerous predator, preferring detritus and very small invertebrates as food. Like most echinoderms it has good regenerative powers, as shown in the specimen at the right. As long as the central disc is intact the animal will survive almost anything. Photo at right by W. Deas, that below by J. Mougin, courtesy Dr. D. Terver, Nancy Aquarium, France.

In some areas starfishes or seastars literally stand out from their surroundings, seemingly offering perfect targets for any passing predator. However, few animals eat starfishes because they are composed mostly of calcareous plates covered with spiny skin. The tissues often have large concentrations of iodine and other unusual elements, making them unpalatable to virtually all fishes and most carnivorous mollusks. Not all starfishes have large tube feet and are active predators on bivalves. Some, like these *Fromia monilis*, have only small tube feet and are relatively inactive, feeding mostly on detritus and small invertebrates in the substrate. Photo by Dr. Herbert R. Axelrod.

shed parts or all of their long, slender arms when disturbed, although they grow them again. For this reason, and because they hide away most of the time, they are not good aquarium animals. However, they feed readily and learn to emerge when food appears— not dried food, but frozen foods or chopped up clam. Some of the largest species such as *Ophiarachnella,* are not brittle and capture prey by quickly coiling an arm or arms around it and scuttle around the tank like a spider. One I have had for a long time now fights a running battle with its fishy tank-mates. It *may* have caught one or two small fishes that have disappeared in a large tank with lots of cover where a death may go undetected, but with the corpse no trouble as there are plenty of invertebrates to dispose of it. It certainly loses out to the larger angels who constantly bite off the ends of its arms as rapidly as it regrows them.

The feather stars, or crinoids, have large feathery arms and a small central disc provided with *cirri,* hook-like structures by which the star affixes itself to the reef or other structure. They are filter feeders and can move around when adult, but go through a stalked stage of development, reminding us of their derivation from the "sea lilies" that abounded in earlier oceans and were deep water forms. Feather stars are brittle and must be handled carefully. They are also poor companions to fishes, that tend to pick them to pieces.

At first sight, sea urchins with their spherical bodies and usually prominent spines do not

The blue starfish or seastar, *Linckia laevigata,* is often kept in the aquarium and provides a truly startling sight. Unfortunately they are hard to feed because they are mostly detritus gatherers. Notice that the number of arms varies. Photo by Dr. Herbert R. Axelrod.

Left: The crown of thorns starfish, *Acanthaster plancii*, is usually a secretive animal, but it has had periods of tremendous population explosions when it has heavily decimated its principal prey, stony corals. Photo by R. Jonklaas.

Below: Hundreds of starfishes can survive in the aquarium, but few are available commercially. This *Anthenea crassa* from the Great Barrier Reef is not unattractive and probably would do well in the aquarium. Photo by R. Steene.

Flattened sea urchins are called sand dollars. Some species are attractive and can be fun to watch as they glide across the aquarium bottom. The *Brissus latecarinatus* above is a burrowing sand dollar or sea biscuit (because of its general shape) that is active mainly at night. The more typical sand dollar below is the common eastern North American *Mellita quinquiesperforata*, often found cast up on beaches. Photo above by S. Johnson, that below by N. Herwig.

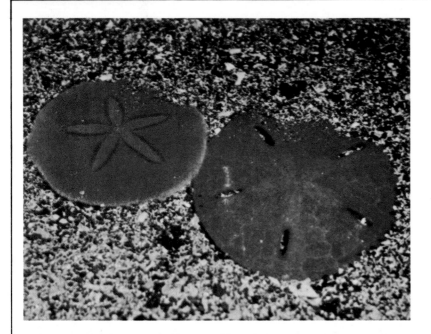

resemble starfishes, but they are built on the same pattern. Imagine a starfish with its arms folded up and joined together so as to form a ball, you then have a sea urchin in essence. In the urchins, there is added calcification to a greater extent than in other echinoderms, so that the dead skeleton is still a hollow ball. Most urchins are scavengers and omnivorous in diet. They fare well in the aquarium as long as algae are present. Some are venomous and all should be handled with care as spines broken off in the flesh can cause festering sores. Sand dollars are flattened urchins that inhabit sandy areas and are of little attraction.

Sea cucumbers look just as their name suggests, at least most of them do. Many are just slug-like, dull cylinders with a head at one end that is just an opening surrounded by short tentacles and an anus at the other. Some are quite gorgeous, brightly colored and attractive, with feathery tentacles gathering in particles of food. A dull genus is *Holothuria,* that burrows in sand and exists on debris. A brilliant family is the Dendrochirotidae, that feed on plankton, but need a lot of it to thrive in the aquarium.

Sea urchins come in a variety of shapes and colors. The sand dollars (top left) are flattened and often show the five-parted symmetry of their group only in the tube foot rows that form a flower-shaped figure at the center of the disc. More typical urchins have long or short spines on a spherical or nearly spherical body. The spines are brittle and break off readily in the skin when stepped on or handled. Photo of *Astriclypeus manni* (solid) and *Scaphechinus mirabilis* (perforated) at top left by Takemura and Susuki; that of *Centrostephanus coronatus* at middle by D. Gotshall; *Diadema setosum* at bottom by A. Power. Facing page: a colorful diademid urchin.

Most sea cucumbers actually look like cucumbers, rather stout and prickly. Although this specimen has a pleasing color pattern, it has the typical disadvantages of its group: it is secretive, a burrower, has poisonous secretions, and is exceedingly slimy on occasion.

Holothuria and related genera of sea cucumbers are marginally satisfactory aquarium inhabitants. Some have attractive colors and patterns (leading to common names such as sea apple and sea pear). Photo by A. Norman.

MOLLUSCA

This is a very large phylum with a host of aquarium representatives. They are characterized by having a shell, not always obvious but usually visible externally and forming a protection for the animal. There is often an eye-bearing head and an organ, the radula, with which the mollusk rasps away its food. Mollusks come in a great variety of types, from snails to octopuses and so defy too general a description.

The univalves or snail-like mollusks with a single shell abound in the ocean. Limpet-like forms crawl over the surface of rocks feeding on vegetation and usually having a home "base" to which they retire when at rest. They are easy to keep and resist predation. Cowries, genus *Cypraea,* are often pretty and worth keeping, as part of their flesh, the mantle, flows over the shell when they are active and is sometimes brightly colored, while the shell itself may be nicely patterned. Beware of whelk-like creatures that are predatory mainly on other mollusks, and of cone shells, that are poisonous and predatory. Some are poisonous to humans, too.

Nudibranchs, sea hares, and similar mollusks are univalves with the shell buried permanently under the skin or even absent. The sea hares, genus *Tethys* and others, feed on algae and will live in the aquarium, but the nudibranchs, with a waving external gill or gills on their backs or around the anus are specialist carnivores, feeding on sometimes bizarre prey such as the Portuguese man-of-war *(Physalia),* or sponges, hydroids

Cowries are attractive and inoffensive mollusks that often do very well in aquaria that can provide enough algal growth to support their constant rasping on the sides and bottom. A few learn to take small pieces of sea-food. Photo *Cypraea zebra* above by C. Arneson; that of *Cypraea cribraria* below by R. Steene.

1

2

Photos 1, 2, 3: Many people collect cowry shells but never see the interesting patterns of the mantle of the living animal. The tiger cowry, *Cypraea tigris*, is often available. The animal shown is spreading the mantle over the shell (from left to right). Photos by A. Power.

Above: Flame scallops (*Lima*) sometimes lose much of their bright colors when kept in the aquarium for long periods. Perhaps their natural food is responsible for their colors. Photo by Dr. Herbert R. Axelrod.

Below: The brilliant red colors of a *Lima scabra* in its natural habitat lead to its common name of flame scallop. These are very active swimming mollusks that take many small foods. Photo by C. Arneson.

3

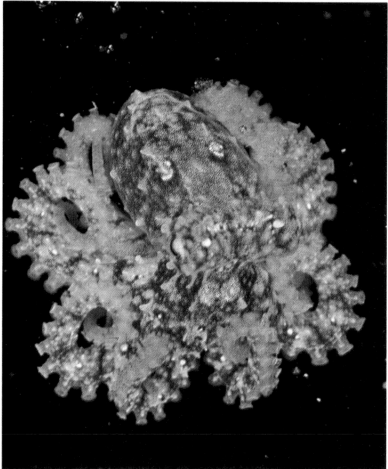

or anemones. Attractive as many of them are, they are therefore condemned to slow starvation in most aquaria.

The bivalves have a hinged shell and include clams, scallops, and mussels, all common aquarium species, but often not well looked after. They are filter feeders and need a supply of plankton or suitable substitutes such as "invertebrate food" or clam juices. Some clams, like the giants, have in-dwelling algae and will flourish if well illuminated. Clams are sedentary, but the scallops are active, moving around by flapping the shell or by jetting water from around the hinges. The most popular scallop is *Lima,* red or pink in color with a fringe of long tentacles around the shell.

The cephalopods, squids, octopuses, etc., are highly developed, often intelligent mollusks. They are also escape artists and hard to keep confined to the aquarium, particularly octopuses. They are predatory, feeding on anything they can catch and if disturbed liable to flood the water with their ink, a dark fluid that acts as a camouflage while its producer escapes. Finally, some are poisonous and can inflict painful or even fatal bites. So *you* choose whether to keep one!

Cephalopods are mollusks in which the creeping foot of the familiar snail is divided into eight or ten arms. Squid such as the *Sepioteuthis* at the top have ten arms, *Octopus* and its relatives (bottom) have eight. Photo at top by C. Arneson, that at bottom by Dr. T. E. Thompson.

Although few cephalopods are kept in the aquarium, several are available and make attractive and very interesting additions. Recently a few species of cuttle-fish from the tropics have been bred in the larger public aquaria, so eventually young *Sepia* like the one above may become available to aquarists. They would make active and colorful additions to any tank. Most octopuses available commercially are rather dull and delicate, but some are more colorful and hardy. *Octopus ornatus* (below) sometimes is available as small specimens and does moderately well in an established aquarium. Photo above by G. Smit, that below by S. Johnson.

Foods and Feeding

There are two ways, among many others, in which fishes differ from land vertebrates. The first is that they convert food to flesh much more efficiently and so need less to put on a given amount of body weight. Wild animals and man turn about 10% of their food to flesh, domestic animals bred for high yield do better at up to 30%, trout and salmon 50% or better. Presumably marine fishes in general do as well, but we don't know for certain. The second is that a starved juvenile mammal or bird is very miserable and skinny but a fish kept on a restricted diet when growing up just stays small, but doesn't look starved. Underfed once it is adult it will of course go thin, as its skeleton cannot shrink down to a smaller size.

In such studies as have been made, it turns out that the warmer the water, the higher the protein requirements of fishes. At 45°F, salmon need

Over the last decade or so many new manufacturers of greatly improved marine diets have been providing hobbyists with excellent foods for all their fishes and invertebrates. No longer are marine foods just the usual dried brine shrimp and flour paste flakes. Today's foods are scientifically designed and provide a balanced diet for almost any animal that adapts to captivity. Your pet shop is always the first place to look for the best food for your pets.

40% protein for best growth, at 58°F they need 55%. Marine fishes need more protein than freshwater ones, so tropical marines really do need a high protein diet. (The percentages quoted are those of the *dry* weight of food, as in flakes or freeze-dried products. Wet weight percentages as in fresh chopped prawns or meat will be around ¼ or less of the dry weight). Aim for 45% protein or more in any dried food you purchase. Many fall below this requirement. The rest will be carbohydrate and fat, plus a little ash, and as long as the fat is not saturated, as are most red meat fats, it doesn't much matter how much there is.

Remember that the more you feed, the fewer fishes your aquarium can hold, because its total capacity to deal with waste products is fixed.

A given amount of food adds so much to the burden on the filter whether it passes through one fish or twenty fishes. While not starving the fishes, do not feed excessively even if they will eat it, remember the two facts in the first paragraph.

DIETARY DIFFERENCES

Some fishes are vegetarians and feed on algae in the wild - surgeons are a good example. Others are strictly carnivorous, such as lionfishes and triggerfishes. Most are omnivorous and eat a mixed diet, while yet others are such specialist feeders that they are difficult to maintain. It pays to ask your dealer what a particular fish has been eating and to let you see it feed. If he has not accustomed it to a readily obtainable food, think twice before you buy it. Young

fishes often accept brine shrimp or small plankton whereas the adults of the same species may not, so be prepared to accommodate your purchases as they grow up. Be especially careful with young angels or chaetodons, some species can be really difficult.

It is important to offer as varied a diet as your fishes will accept, so that any deficiency in one item may, we hope, be made up by another. A mixed tank of fishes and perhaps invertebrates should be given a mixture of foods each day, either by preparing mixed batches or giving several different foods in small amounts rather than any one food exclusively. We do not know enough about the detailed dietary requirements of fishes to claim that any one food is adequate, particularly in relation to vitamins and minerals.

VEGETABLE FOODS

A well-matured aquarium has sufficient algae growing in it to provide much of the needs of vegetarians. This means not only the encrusting algae that cover the glass and coral or rocks, but at least filamentous algae that grow even in moderate light. If you can cultivate some of the *Caulerpa* species or other green algae offered by dealers, so much the better. It is a good sign if, in addition, your algal growth is so lush that you have to crop some of it yourself, as the removal of excess algae is the removal of waste products. Use a commercial algal food in the recommended amounts if it seems to be needed. Such "foods" are mineral mixes that stimulate growth, sometimes with added vitamins as well.

If you have a lot of vegetarians and poor algal growth, feed deep- frozen lettuce, spinach or other suitable plant material, even peas or green beans, all chopped to a suitable size. The freezing process does no harm and makes them more acceptable to most fishes. You can add special vegetarian flakes as well. It is not advisable to feed algae fresh from the ocean because of the danger of disease, but dried seaweed as offered in health stores or Oriental shops is good.

LIVE ANIMAL FOODS

The live foods given to freshwater fishes are mostly suitable for marines as they will live long enough to be eaten. Some such as the insect larvae will live for hours if left to do so. It is best not to feed unsterilized foods from marine sources because of the danger of disease, but a dunk in fresh water for a few minutes will clean up most of them. Filter feeders like clams or mussels probably carry the greatest danger.

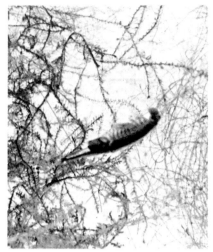

Small crustaceans are the best foods for many fishes and invertebrates. Almost any shrimp, amphipod, isopod, mysid shrimp, or their relatives will be taken by the active predators in your marine aquarium. Even freshwater crustaceans can be fed to marine fishes, although most will not survive long in salt water. Photo by C. O. Masters.

Live foods promote active feeding in many fishes and often help bring out the best colors. However, many species will readily adapt to scientifically designed prepared foods. Art by J. R. Quinn.

WORMS

For all fishes, white worms, *Enchytraeus albidus,* are fine as occasional foods, as is the smaller Grindal worm. Don't feed them frequently as they are full of saturated fats. They can be cultured in soil with pockets of porridge or other milky breakfast foods, covered with glass and kept in the dark by another cover if necessary.

Tubificid worms *(Tubifex,* etc.) well cleaned by washing for hours or days under a dripping tap may be purchased as another treat, with the same warning. They can be very useful for tempting fussy eaters. Earthworms, whole or chopped, can also be purchased if need be, and make a fine meal for the larger fish. If collecting them yourself, avoid the smelly, yellow dung worm.

INSECT LARVAE

Mosquito larvae make excellent food, not using up oxygen and remaining available if uneaten immediately. If left too long they may change into pupae and hatch out, but this is very unlikely in the marine aquarium. They can also be stored in screw-top jars in the refrigerator without losing much of their nutritive value. *Chironomus,* the "bloodworm", is a large red larva of a gnat, less frequently encountered, but excellent food. *Chaoborus,* the "glassworm", is a colorless relative and equally good.

Mealworms, beetle larvae, as used by fishermen, and blowfly maggots are much enjoyed by large fishes and can be chopped up and washed for the smaller ones. These larvae tend to be fatty, however, so their use should be restricted.

BRINE SHRIMP

The brine shrimp, *Artemia salina,* is an excellent fish food and may be purchased as dried eggs, to be fed to small fishes after hatching, as live adults, or as frozen adults. They are, in one form or another, the commonest food after flakes. The dried eggs hatch out in seawater or "seawater" made from artificial salts and are readily available. For small batches, they may be floated on the surface of the water in a shallow dish, not more than one half teaspoon per gallon. They will hatch in 48 hours or so at 70°F, in 24 hours at 80°F, but will not hatch in cold water. The newly hatched larvae *(nauplii)* are attracted to light soon after hatching and can be siphoned off with care from the lighter side of the dish, or you can siphon the lot, taking care to leave the floating shells behind. For larger batches, use a different method. Set up gallon jars with aeration and fill about ¾ with salt water. Use up to 1 teaspoon per gallon of eggs and keep them briskly aerated until hatching, then turn off the air and leave to settle. Some egg shells will float, some will sink, but the free-swimming nauplii can be siphoned off as before.

Your local pet shop will have a food to fit all your needs. Remember that there is no single food that will suit all your animals at all times of their lives. Specialty foods are necessary for some animals and some situations, such as feeding breeding fishes or feeding corals and similar animals. Your pet dealer will recommend the proper food for your requirements.

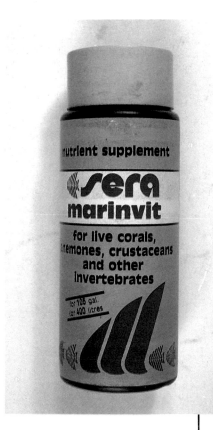

You can grow the shrimp by transferring about 500 per gallon to a stronger brine, which for San Francisco shrimp should be made of 10 oz common salt, 2 oz Epsom salts and 1 oz of baking powder or bicarbonate of soda, per gallon. Feed them on baker's yeast, just a pinch at a time, to be repeated when the brine clears. See that the yeast is thoroughly mixed with a little brine before adding it to the culture. The shrimp will become adult and breed in 6 - 8 weeks at about 75°F, producing eggs that hatch without drying. Utah and other types of *Artemia* need different brines, usually specified by the supplier, or may grow in double strength sea water, some even in straight sea water. Brine shrimp eggs may be purchased already shelled and may then be placed straight into the aquarium to be eaten or to hatch.

A balanced diet is just as necessary for your fishes as it is for you. Fishes may not need the same food groups as humans or cattle, but they should have a selection of living and prepared food available, preferably fed in alternation. Although most fishes will survive on just manufactured food or just brine shrimp, it is always best to offer a variety. Art by J. R. Quinn.

Do not overlook the potential of locally collected foods. These shield shrimp, *Triops*, would be taken readily by many larger marine fishes and would provide good nourishment. Be careful of contamination of the aquarium with small pests and predators, as well as parasites. Photo by U. E. Friese.

Brine shrimp, *Artemia*, are considered by many to be the ultimate live food for marine animals. Photo compliments of San Francisco Bay Brand, Inc.

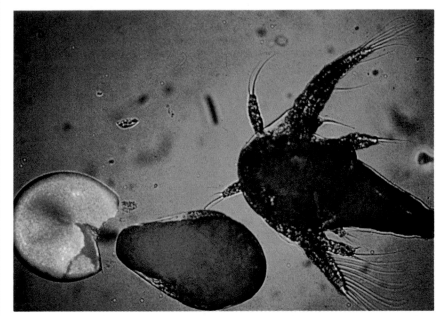

From the moment of hatching (above) to maturity (below, a male), the brine shrimp is edible by the majority of aquarium fishes and most of the invertebrates. They can be cultured at home or purchased live, frozen, or dried. Photos courtesy Artemia Reference Center.

Few aquarists fail to have a can or two of brine shrimp eggs on hand for emergencies, such as feeding an unexpected batch of fry.

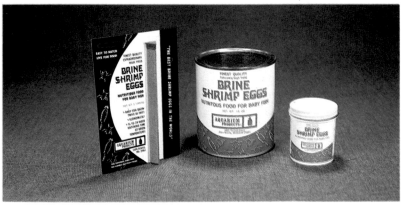

➤ If you have the time and inclination, you often can collect your own foods. Remember that many marine fishes and invertebrates will readily take freshwater animals as food with no questions asked. Be careful of introducing parasites and pests into the aquarium, a risk that is reduced when introducing freshwater food animals to marine tanks. Art by J. R. Quinn.

  a. Daphnia
  b. Copepod
  c–e. Rotifers
  f. Tubificid worms
  g. Bloodworm
  h. Glassworm
  i–j. Earthworms
  k. Brine shrimp

➤ Collecting gear can be as simple or complex as you wish, either purchased or homemade. Some typical collecting gear used by experienced collectors includes:

  l. Dip net
  m. Carrying jar
  n. Sieve
  o. Filtering jar
  p. Sieve carrier

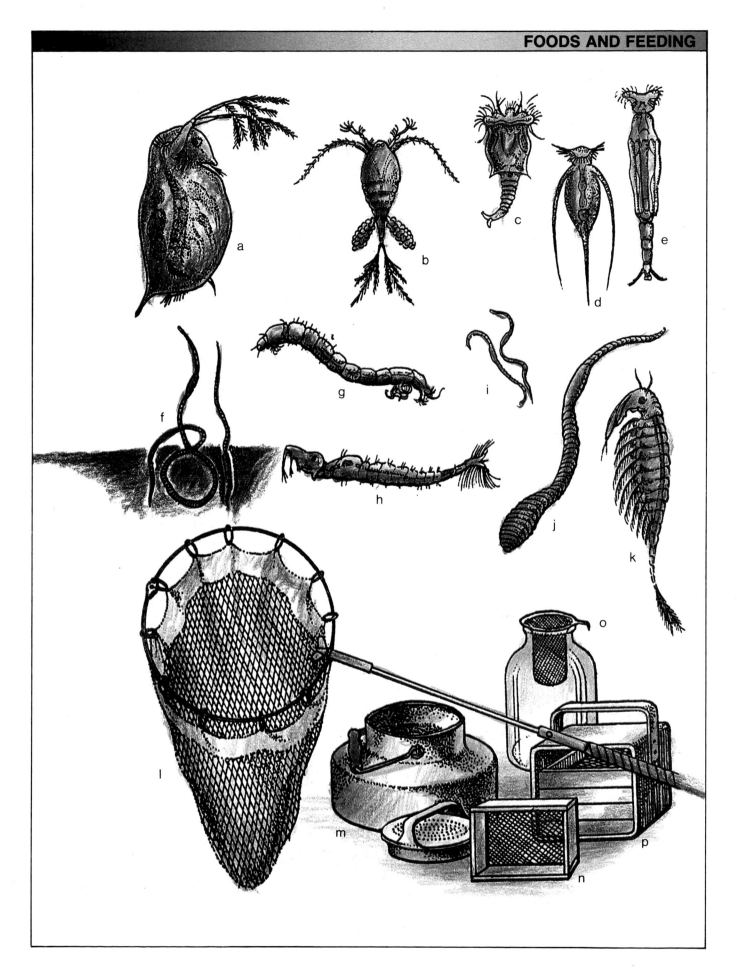

a

b

c

d

e

f

g

h

i

j

k

l

m

n

o

p

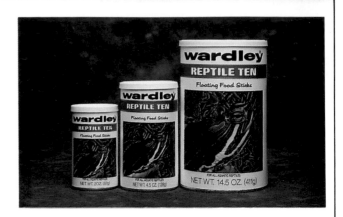

A basic diet of prepared foods suitable for most fishes and other aquatic animals, such as turtles, could include a basic staple food plus such items as a cichlid food (includes a variety of plant and animal ingredients) and even a turtle food (includes fish meal, algae, bloodworms, etc.)

If you can supplement this type of diet with regular feedings of live foods such as daphnia most fishes should thrive in your aquarium if all other conditions are correct. Photo of daphnia by A. Untergasser.

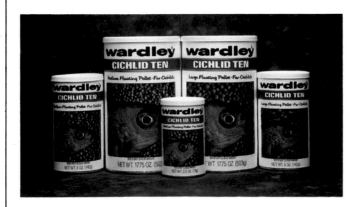

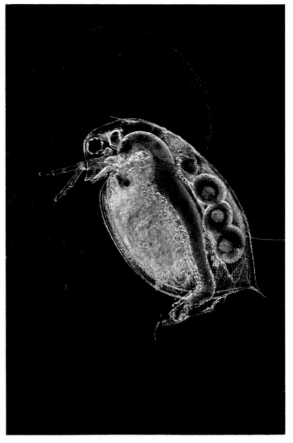

WATER FLEAS

The water flea, *Daphnia pulex,* is not often for sale, but can be collected from ponds in summer with a fine net. It can be seen as brown, reddish or green swarms in mid-water, depending on the strain of flea and its diet. It is a good food, having a hard shell that stimulates the gut and will often survive for hours in sea water. It does not breed readily in small vessels, but can be raised in tubs of 50 gallons or more, kept fairly cool and fed on liver powder, dried blood, or other rich foods, preferably with aeration.

Other small crustaceans such as *Cyclops, Moina,* and *Diaptomus* may be collected similarly, so may larger freshwater shrimps. If you live near the sea, you can make similar collections from tide pools, of an almost endless variety of larval forms and small adults, but wash them well in fresh water before feeding to your fishes.

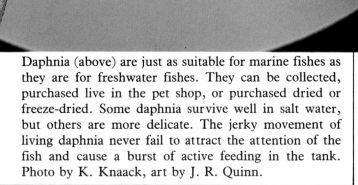

Daphnia (above) are just as suitable for marine fishes as they are for freshwater fishes. They can be collected, purchased live in the pet shop, or purchased dried or freeze-dried. Some daphnia survive well in salt water, but others are more delicate. The jerky movement of living daphnia never fail to attract the attention of the fish and cause a burst of active feeding in the tank. Photo by K. Knaack, art by J. R. Quinn.

FROZEN FOODS

Next best to live foods are the frozen foods, in particular those that have been sterilized by irradiation. They retain all the "goodness" and are free of diseases or parasites. Most fishes enjoy them as readily as the live originals. The commonest is brine shrimp, followed by mysid and other shrimps, often sold as "krill." Take care that these have not been thawed and refrozen, sometimes more than once, as they may then have become a useless soup that merely pollutes the water. Other frozen preparations are of tiny fishes, beef heart, mollusks of various types, plankton—almost any type of food you may wish for, but not always available. Most aquarium shops also carry frozen foods.

DRIED FOODS

Many of the live or frozen foods mentioned can also be obtained freeze-dried or just merely dried. They are then concentrated and should be fed correspondingly sparingly. Some aquarists soak them before feeding, but the fishes seem to prefer the unsoaked article. Dried tubifex, bloodworms, krill, and the like offer the high protein diet recommended for tropical marines, but one wonders about their vitamin content. It is probably best to add a vitamin preparation if using much of this type of food.

Dry food in flake, granule or pellet form often has vitamins added and can form a reasonable part of the total diet, but best not more than 50%. Special flakes for marine fishes are available, that should contain not less than 45% protein, except in the case of vegetarian flakes, which necessarily have less. The colors of flakes are usually there to please the aquarist and mean nothing, but there are brands which are color-coded as to contents. As with other dry foods, flakes are concentrated and must not be overfed, or they can swell in the fishes' tummies and cause distress.

Granular foods can offer the larger fishes more than flakes, and may contain recognizable pieces of roe, insects, and crustaceans that cannot go into flakes. Don't use pond foods that contain very low protein percentages meant for cold-water fishes like goldfish.

DOMESTIC FOODS

Many of the foods we eat are good for fishes, seafoods particularly. Fresh shrimps, crab, lobster, shellfish of all types, squid, and the less oily fishes are all good foods, preferably washed in fresh water first to eliminate possible sources of disease as far as it can be done. Canned foods can be used as well as the fresh ones, if also well washed. Chop the food up into suitable sizes for your particular fishes. To them can be added frozen vegetables as already mentioned.

As any schoolboy knows, fishes like bread and bread is good for them in moderation, containing roughage and vitamins as well as vegetable matter. To my surprise, I found that various Pacific angelfishes take it readily, even ones that refuse dry foods. On reflection, I wonder if it looks like the sponges on which many of

Your local pet shop is always the best place to start looking for the best foods for your fishes. Prepared foods are nutritious and convenient and are readily accepted by most fishes.

them feed in nature? Brown bread seems the most attractive, which is excellent! Anemonefishes, in contrast, won't touch it.

FEEDING STRATEGIES

As we have seen, many marine fishes are aggressive and they are frequently more intelligent than freshwater fishes. The result is that the belligerent ones will chase the others away at feeding time if allowed the chance to do so successfully, which is the case if you feed slowly and at one spot. It is better to scatter the food a bit, having chopped it into a suitable range of sizes for all fishes present, and to feed quite a bit at once. Flakes will spread over the surface and so do not present much difficulty, so will most other dry foods. Don't put frozen blocks into the

If you feed live foods such as tubificid worms, you probably should use a feeding ring or feeding trap. These simple plastic and cork gadgets concentrate the food long enough that the fishes get a chance to pick at it before the worms make it to the bottom of the tank and hide in the substrate. Never put a feeding ring near the territory of a dominant male as he may keep all other fishes from feeding in his territory. Art by J. R. Quinn.

tank as this defeats the object of making the food readily available to all; a hungry large fish will swallow quite a large frozen chunk in one gulp - rather like swallowing a pint of ice cream, but it doesn't seem to worry them.

The problem can be exaggerated with invertebrates present and care has to be taken to see that all of them get fed. Filter feeders are a difficulty sometimes, but the advice some authors give to remove them from the tank for feeding is not realistic as it is usually impossible to follow. Just make up your mind to cloud the water with a suitable suspension of invertebrate food and perhaps turn off filters for half an hour. Suitable foods are commercially available or may be made by shaking up mashed egg yolk, brains, liver, or such in sea water and straining off coarse material before feeding. Live foods such as newly hatched brine shrimp are of course excellent, as are any dry foods intended for freshwater fishes.

Most fishes rest at night while many invertebrates roam around, so this is the time to feed the latter. Just chop suitable small bits of clam, crab, fish, etc. for the crustaceans and some echinoderms. Drop pieces onto the anemones, or teach them, by repeated attempts, to accept pieces thrust into their mouths so that nobody else steals them before they are ingested. This can be achieved by brushing the food on the end of a fine probe gently against the tentacles for a few seconds, then placing it into the mouth. Later, it can go straight in and will be accepted. Do all this with a light two or three times a week and your invertebrates will flourish. You can feed the filter feeders at the same time if you wish, but this is not necessary. If you do, remember to switch the filters on again if you turned them off.

Freeze-dried foods of all types are suitable for marine aquaria. Although zooplankton may seem more "natural" to the fish than mosquito larvae, remember that the fish probably recognize food more by smell and chemistry than appearance.

This *Pomacanthus semicirculatus* obviously has a bad and perhaps fatal case of marine white spot, *Cryptocaryon*. The first question that should be asked is not how the white spot got into the tank, but what stressed the fish so severely that it became infected to such an extent in the first place. The mere presence of a disease agent in the aquarium does not mean that the fish will become infected. Stress is the killer of aquarium fishes, so the first thing to look for at the outbreak of a disease is the cause of the stress. Most diseases can be cured or controlled, but any cure is only temporary as long as the sources of stress remain. Photo by Frickhinger.

Troubles

If the recommendations already given are followed, troubles should be few and far between, but nothing works perfectly and even if you have followed them meticulously, upsets can occur. Despite quarantine, no tank is sterile and freedom from stress or disease is always a relative business. Compared with the ocean, any aquarium is vastly overcrowded and once an infection or parasite gets going the fishes are likely to need assistance. However, they do have their own immune systems and in a well-kept aquarium an infection may be present but never become serious. The biggest dangers are to newly introduced fishes that may fall prey to something already in the tank to which they have no immunity, and to the old inhabitants if a new fish brings in something to which *they* are not immune. Quarantine can only eliminate certain conditions, mainly external parasites, and give you an opportunity to recognize the presence of others.

Conditions predisposing to disease are overcrowding, poor feeding and maintenance, and lack of reasonable precautions when adding fishes (or invertebrates) to the tank. Overcrowding and overfeeding will be likely to cause a rise in ammonia production beyond the capacity of the filter. This weakens the fishes and they fall sick with anything that crops up, just as in the new tank syndrome. Poor maintenance can have the same effect, causing accumulations of

Defective water chemistry is the prime cause of aquarium stress, so it is essential that the hobbyist always be aware of any swings in ammonia and nitrite levels, for instance, in the aquarium. Many good testing kits are available that allow rapid and simple tests to be run to check water quality on a regular basis. Regular testing for at least ammonia, nitrite, and nitrate levels plus salinity is greatly to be desired.

ammonia, nitrites and even nitrates beyond tolerable limits, as well as of toxins produced by clogged filters or unremoved by adequate water changes. Stress can add its toll as well, arising from the above or from injudicious choice of tankmates.

DETECTION AND TREATMENT OF DISEASE

The commonly recognized diseases of aquarium fishes are naturally those that cause visible symptoms externally, whether physical or behavioral. Some of these can be cured or alleviated fairly readily, while others warn the aquarist to get rid of the fish suffering from them or risk infecting the rest. If a disease requires skilled diagnoses or laboratory tests for recognition, it too will fall into the "get rid of" category for the average aquarist unless the whole tank is infected and hit or miss methods are applied.

If the aquarist has no quarantine facilities or a particular fish is difficult to catch without wrecking the decor, it may be necessary to treat the whole tank even if it is preferable to medicate the individual fish. The same is true if there is a likelihood that the rest of the fishes may be infected even if not yet showing signs of it. When it *is* necessary to treat the tank as a whole, nobody wants to use a medicine that will stain fitments, color the water deeply, or kill the nitrifying bacteria in the biological filter. So these treatments will be recommended only if nothing else will do, or if the fish can be isolated. The biggest danger of in-tank treatment is damage to

Your pet shop has everything you need to test the water, change the water chemistry, and even change the biology of the tank.

the biological filter, which cannot be turned off for long and so must be subjected to the substance used. Carbon filters must usually be turned off during treatment as they remove medications, but that does them no harm unless a large, old filter has been allowed to become biological, a point to remember, as a severely affected biological filter poisons the water.

When a fish is sick, remember that not all sickness is caused by disease or parasites. The fish may be suffering from poisoning due to bad maintenance or the introduction of a poison such as fly spray to the tank. It may be suffering from malnutrition, bullying, or even from a genetic (inborn) condition that is incurable, such as a tumor or curved spine, although both can have other causes. So if you don't see specific signs of disease or parasites, think of other things that may be wrong before applying a "cure" that may only make matters worse. Call in an experienced marine aquarist, if you can, to help with a diagnosis, or your local vet, who is becoming more and more likely to be able to offer help.

There are many proprietory remedies on the shelves intended for freshwater fishes that are not particularly suitable for marines, and those that are seem usually to be mixed preparations at a rather low individual dosage. Hence it is best to use pure chemicals as recommended in this chapter, or at least to make sure that whatever is in a remedy is as recommended here. Copper-containing preparations, for instance, are most often of

chelated copper that stays around for months and is very difficult to eliminate from a tank and equally difficult to assay for controlling the concentration in the water. When using any remedy, calculate the actual volume of water as accurately as you can; it will be less than the theoretical capacity of the tank, quite a bit less in small tanks. This is done by subtracting from the height the average depth of the gravel plus the air space on top, then multiplying the result by 0.95 to allow for the volume of coral and rocks etc. Thus, the theoretical volume of a 36″ x 16″ x 20″ tank is 36 x 16 x 20/231 = 49.9 gals., whereas the corrected estimate is, say, 36 x 16 x 16/231 x 0.95 = 37.9 gals., quite a difference!

More specialized testing kits are also available at your pet shop. If you suspect, for instance that copper may be killing your shrimp, your dealer will have a simple test for the problem...and a cure.

Symptoms

Here is a table of the symptoms exhibited by fishes

suffering from some of the commoner troubles. It will help in deciding what is probably wrong, then reading up the more detailed account of each condition will help further. If you end up not at all sure, you can treat for two or three possibilities at once, first making certain that the drugs to be given do not interact by mixing some together at the dosages stated in a small vessel. If no precipitate, cloudiness, or color change occurs, go ahead.

VIRAL DISEASES

Viruses are sub-microscopic parasites of cells, incapable of reproduction on their own, known to cause many diseases in higher vertebrates but little studied in fishes.

Lymphocystis virus causes cells to swell enormously and groups of them become tumors composed of connective tissue, at first looking rather like a fluffy fungus, later like tapioca on skin or fins, later still like tiny cauliflowers up to ½" or so in size. There is no certain cure, but the disease may become self-limiting. However, it is best to destroy an infected fish as the virus spreads rapidly to others.

Lateral line disease is thought to be due to a virus and is sometimes cured by a change of environment. It rarely affects more than one or two fishes in a tank and seems to be of low grade infectivity. There is no specific cure. The disease usually starts at the head and progresses down the lateral line, giving it a channelled-out look.

Symptoms and Probable Causes

Symptom	Probable Cause
Small white spots on body or fins, fins clamped, glancing off coral, etc.	Cryptocaryon irritans (white spot)
Very small white spots giving velvety appearance, behavior as above	Amyloodinum ocellatum (velvet or coral fish disease)
No small spots, but behavior as above	Toxic conditions
Small white spots that come and go	Gyrodactylus or other flukes
White or gray fluffy patches	Lymphocystis (a virus)
White or gray flat patches	Chondrococcus columnaris
Whitish nodules, "cauliflower" growths on skin	Lymphocystis
White or dark nodules under the skin	Plistophora, Glugea, Henneguya or cestode larvae
Red streaks on skin or fins, ulcers	Vibrio or other bacteria
Rotting of tail or fins	Vibrio, Pseudomonas
Ulceration of skin, yellow or darker nodules on or below skin	Ichthyosporidium (a fungus)
Wasting, hollow belly, possibly sores	Mycobacterium marinum (tuberculosis) or starvation
Scale protrusion, often reddish, with normal body	Bacterial infection of scales, probably Vibrio
Scale protrusion due to body swelling	Dropsy, probably Cornyebacterium
Pop-eye (exophthalmos)	Gas embolism, copper poisoning, possibly bacterial
Cloudy eyes or blindness	Toxins, severe white spot, or velvet
Unusual or very dark coloration	Toxins, Ichthyosporidium, or nervous system disturbance
Fins constantly erect	Sign of impending death
Loss of balance, sluggishness	Water too cold, possibly disease

Severe loss of balance, upside-down	Swim bladder disease
Gasping at surface	Water too hot, O_2 lack or CO_2 excess, toxins
Sudden dashes, even out of water	Low pH, lice or flukes, toxins
Destruction of lateral line	Probably a virus
Spinal curvature	Tuberculosis, *Ichthyosporidium,* vitamin or calcium lack, genetic
Visible external crustaceans on skin	Copepods *(Argulus* etc.)

A severe case of lateral line disease in the tang *Zebrasoma desjardini.* Seldom do cases of this mysterious disease progress so far. Many treatments have been attempted, mostly without success, but occasionally the condition spontaneously cures itself. Photo by Dr. Herbert R. Axelrod.

BACTERIAL DISEASES

Bacteria are more advanced than viruses and can multiply on their own, but cause many diseases in fishes. There will not often be a chance to determine exactly which species of bacterium is causing a particular condition, however we can often guess from past experience which one it is and treat accordingly.

Red streaks on the body or fins may later proceed to ulcers and loss of finnage parts . It is then called *tail rot* or *fin rot.* The commonest culprits are species of *Pasteurella, Vibrio,* or *Pseudomonas (Aeromonas),* all so-called gram-negative that do not respond to penicillin (although they may to some of the new synthetic pencillins). Treatment of the whole tank is only likely to succeed if the trouble is caught very early, when a good clean up and disinfection with acriflavine (trypaflavine) or monacrin (mono-amino-acridine) may work. Make up either drug as a 0.2% solution in distilled or tap water and give up to 1 teaspoon (5 ml) per gallon, to be repeated as the slight yellow or blue color subsides, usually about every 3 days. If there is no cure after a week, switch to the next treatment.

It is best not to use antibiotics in the aquarium as general treatments because of their relative ineffectiveness in salt water, the danger of culturing resistant strains, and of effects on filters. Instead, give them in the food, in a concentration of about 1%. Chloromycetin, neomycin, or gentamycin are all likely to cure the disease, with preference to the first-named.

The best food to mix with is a flake, but anything the fishes will eat that can be used is acceptable. Feed at least twice a day.

If the fishes are not eating, the whole tank, may as a last resort, have to be treated. If only a few are affected, they may be caught out and treated in isolation. Turn off all filters, aerate briskly, and turn on the biological filter twice a day for ½ hour. Treat the isolated fish with 50 mg per gallon and repeat every 2 days, switching to another drug if ineffective after three treatments.

Tuberculosis causes wasting, hollow belly, ragged fins, and skin blotches; even a deformed spine. A cure is difficult and should only be contemplated with valuable fishes. The causative organism is *Mycobacterium marinum* and is treated with isoniazid, to be fed to the fishes as for an antibiotic, or added to the water at 50 mg per gallon every 3rd day, siphoning off 25% of the water each time. A cure may take 2 months, so it is best to dispose of any but a precious specimen and to look to general hygiene as a preventative.

Dropsy is a swelling of the abdomen usually caused by kidney disease, that in turn leads to accumulation of body fluids. The scales and sometimes even the eyes protrude, but do not look infected. The bacterium responsible is usually a *Corynebacterium,* unique in being gram-positive and sensitive to penicillin or erythromycin. The latter is preferable and should be given

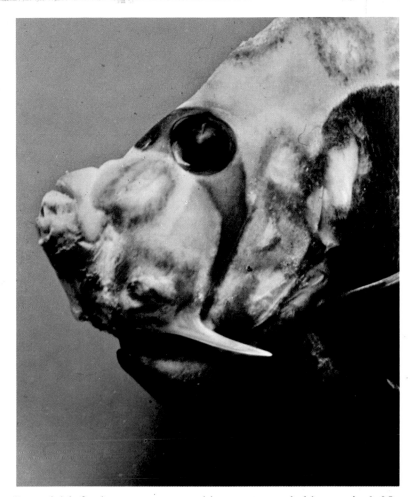

Bacterial infections as severe as this one are probably terminal. Not only is the original infection dangerous, but the sores themselves act as entrance points for still other dangerous bacteria and parasites. In the wild such a fish would have almost no chance of survival, and even in the aquarium it would be best to euthanize it. Photo of *Pomacanthus* by Frickhinger.

by mouth as for other antibiotics, or if absolutely necessary at 50 mg per gallon in the water, repeated every 2 days with 25% removal of water each time.

Distinguish dropsy from scale protrusion, a disease of the scales and skin caused by *Pseudomonas* or other bacteria. There is no swelling of the abdomen, but a reddening around the scales that stick out from the body. Treat as for "red streaks."

Chondrococcus columnaris, which causes "mouth fungus" in freshwater fishes, sometimes infects marines. It then causes grey-white lesions of the skin and fins and should be treated as for "red streaks" also.

PROTOZOAN DISEASES

Protozoa are one-celled animals sometimes large enough to be visible to the naked eye. They are the cause of the most common fish diseases in the aquarium: velvet and white spot.

257

▲ Both broad-spectrum and specific treatments are available at your pet shop. Before treating a disease condition, discuss the problem with your pet dealer to make use of his experience and knowledge.

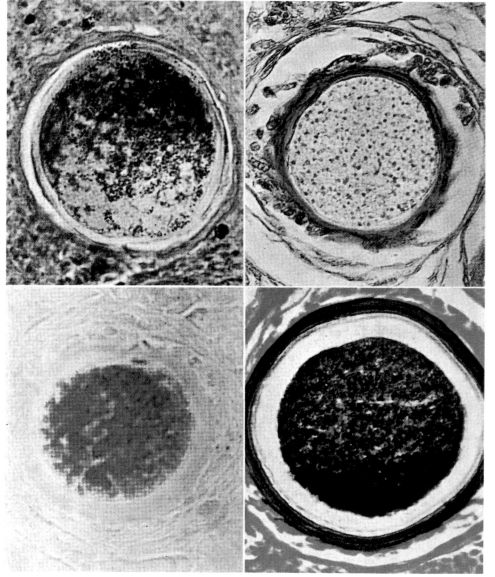

◄ *Ichthyosporidium hoferi*, also known as *Ichthyophonus hoferi*, is a dangerous disease found in both freshwater and marine fishes. The cysts can be found anywhere in the body and cause a variety of symptoms. Photos of various cyst stages and stains by Amlacher.

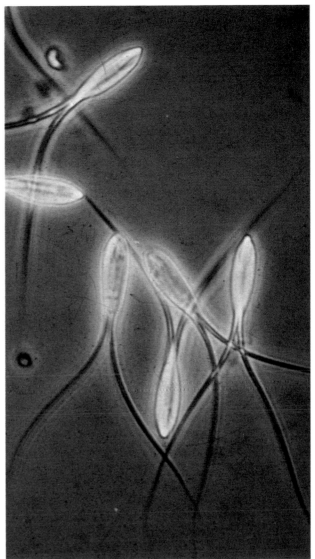

The sporidian *Henneguya* is often seen in marine fishes, where it forms large whitish cysts on the body and fins. There is no reliable treatment, the disease is contagious, and it is terminal, so it is best to euthanize the infected fish. The major problem is that the condition is easily confused with occasionally curable lymphocystis. A microscopic examination of a smear from a cyst will yield sporozoan cells (above) in *Henneguya*, none in lymphocystis. Photos of *Henneguya* cells and an infected *Monodactylus sebae* by Frickhinger.

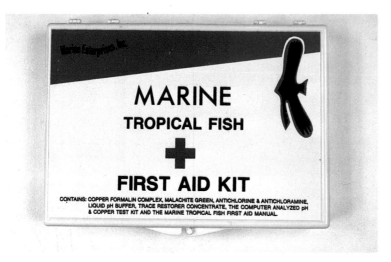

MARINE
TROPICAL FISH
✚
FIRST AID KIT

CONTAINS: COPPER FORMALIN COMPLEX, MALACHITE GREEN, ANTICHLORINE & ANTICHLORAMINE, LIQUID pH BUFFER, TRACE RESTORER CONCENTRATE, THE COMPUTER ANALYZED pH & COPPER TEST KIT AND THE MARINE TROPICAL FISH FIRST AID MANUAL.

The wise aquarist keeps a first aid kit for his aquarium just as you would keep a first aid kit in the bathroom or car. Several good assortments are readily available at your pet shop.

Velvet, or coral fish, disease must always be suspected and can be difficult to detect. It and white spot are the main reasons for a period of quarantine. It shows as a whitish powdery dusting over the surface of the fish and causes rapid respiration due to gill infection and glancing off objects in the tank because of irritation. The cause is *Amyloodinium ocellatum,* which has a free-swimming stage in which it settles onto the fish or in its gills and invades the tissues. There it forms a cyst, embedded in the skin, that drops off after a few days and gives rise to about 200 new infective dinospores - the free-swimming stage. The whole cycle takes about 10 days in the tropical aquarium.

Treatment is best with copper sulphate or copper citrate, the former being easiest to obtain, but the latter is more soluble in sea water. Dosage should be carefully controlled as copper is toxic to fishes as well as to the protozoa. It also kills algae and invertebrates. They should be removed as far as possible from the tank.

It is easiest to treat the whole tank as both it and the fishes must be cleaned up. Make up a 1% solution of the blue copper sulphate crystals in distilled water (tap water may cause a precipitate) and add 0.28 ml per gallon or 5 ml (one standard tea- spoon) per 18 gallons. This gives theoretically 0.15 ppm metallic copper, the recommended dose, but some may be taken up by coral, gravel, etc., and it is therefore best to monitor the actual concentration with a copper test kit. Try to keep it between 0.12 and 0.18 ppm (mg/liter), but if you have no kit, add another dose of copper every three days and keep an eye open for poisoning. Signs of poisoning are gasping, turning onto one side, and exophthalmos (pop-eye). If they appear, turn on the carbon filter or add a suitable

ion exchange resin to any filter. The carbon filter should otherwise be off, but the biological filter can be left on. Although the dose of copper recommended may depress it, it does no severe damage. Treatment must be maintained for at least 10 days; 2 weeks is preferable. The cysts on the fishes will not disappear suddenly, but no more should appear.

White spot is the other very prevalent disease caused by another protozoan, *Cryptocaryon irritans.* The spots are white, larger than velvet, and more easily seen as pinhead cysts imbedded in the skin and fins. They are also present in the gills. There is a free-swimming stage that latches onto the fish, forms the cyst, and soon drops off again. It matures at the bottom of the tank and frees a number of new infective *tomites,* the free-swimming stage. Treatment is exactly the same as for velvet. In the case of both velvet and white spot, an alternative treatment that may be tried in the presence of invertebrates is with quinine. The recommended dosage is 2g of quinine hydrochloride or quinine sulphate, which is less soluble, per 25 gallons, with a 50% change of water on the third day and another half dose of quinine. I would suggest another ½ dose and 50% change on day 6 as well, to continue treatment for an effective period of 10 days.

Sporozoa are protozoa causing a host of regrettably incurable diseases in fishes, at least to date. They are all parasitic.

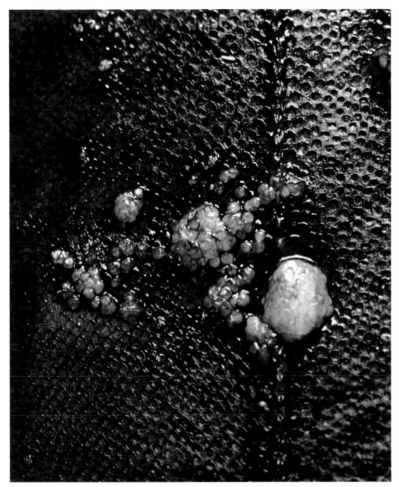

The nodules of lymphocystis are indeed signs of a viral infection, but they also possibly are signs of a poorly run tank.

Carbon filters help remove harmful trace elements and ammonia from the water, reducing stress and the need for chemical treatment of the water.

Those occurring fairly often in aquaria include: *Henneguya,* causing large cysts rather like *Lymphocystis* anywhere on the fish; *Plistophora,* also causing large cysts that form bulges under the skin; and *Glugea,* which causes intramuscular cysts. Any suspected victims are best killed.

FUNGI

Fungi are plants which lack the green pigment, chlorophyll. The main recognized fungal infection in marine fishes is *Ichthyosporidium (Ichthyophonus) hoferi* a common disease of freshwater fishes as well. It is eaten with food or feces, invades the bloodstream and settles down in the liver. From there it spreads everywhere forming cysts up to $1/10''$ in size. Early signs are sluggishness, hollow belly or loss of balance. Later on cysts of a yellow to brown color are seen to appear at the surface of the body. The disease does not kill rapidly and is sometimes self-limiting, but an infected fish should not be left in the aquarium or it will infect others. No sure cure is known, but the addition of phenoxethol or chloromycetin, both at 1% in food, has been recommended (in quarantine, of course) and may be given to a tank from which a sufferer has been removed, as a preventative.

FLUKES

The dangerous marine flukes are those that pass directly from fish to fish. Many other flukes have intermediate hosts such as invertebrates, birds, or mammals and are not often encountered in an aquarium.

Benedenia melleni settles anywhere on the fish and may look like white spot, as it is only 1/6" in size at most. Eggs are laid on the fish and hatch out in about a week as larvae that infect other fishes. In severe infestations, open wounds may result that soon become infected.

Affected fishes scratch themselves on the scenery and behave much as if suffering from white spot, so beware! Cleaners, particularly *Labroides dimidiatus,* the cleaner wrasse, are a great help in preventing the spread of *Benedenia,* but a heavy infestation either involves removal of the fishes and treatment in quarantine with the danger of still having an infected tank, or treatment with a vermicide *in situ.* In quarantine, a one hour bath of one standard teaspoon (5 ml) of concentrated formalin per gallon of salt water should do the trick, or a freshwater bath of up to 10 or 15 minutes (!) at an appropriate pH. The freshwater bath can be tolerated by most fishes, but they must be watched carefully for signs of shock (obvious distress and loss of balance.)

Vermicides to be used in the tank are Dibrom, Dipterex, or Dylox (Trichlorfon) at 0.25 ppm (1 mg per gallon), all of which contain the same preparation, initially an insecticide, DTHP. Don't add them directly to the water, but dissolve them in a gallon or so of aquarium water and stir it gently in, turning off carbon but not biological filters.

Gyrodactylus species are even smaller than *Benedenia,* about 1/25", and very easily mistaken for white spot. Some come and go from the fishes, a good clue to their nature, as white spot stays put. The same treatments as for *Benedenia* are recommended.

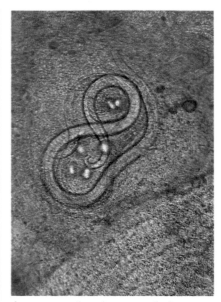

An encapsulated nematode larva. Nematodes seldom are a major problem in marine fishes. Photo by A. Untergasser.

OTHER WORMS

Tapeworms (Cestoda) and round worms (Nematoda) are very common but unrecognized parasites in the gut. Nematodes may be seen at the anus, and can be treated with piperazine at 0.25% in the food for 10 days. Tapeworms, if suspected because of a post-mortem on another fish, can be similarly treated with 0.5% Yomesan as a single dose given after a day's starvation. However, heavily infested fishes can die because a massive death of the worms can block the gut.

Gill flukes often are found on marine fishes but unless they are present in large numbers they are no more than a nuisance. *Gyrodactylus* is one of the more commonly seen genera. Any of several simple chemical treatments will kill all or most of the flukes in the aquarium. Photo by F. Meyer.

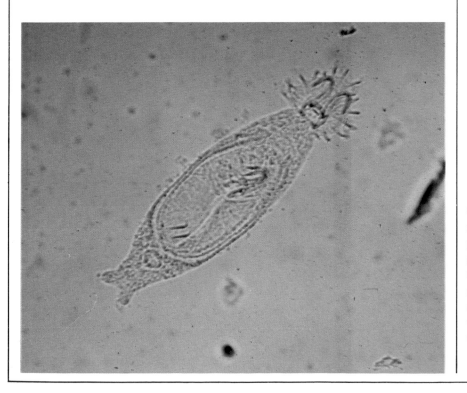

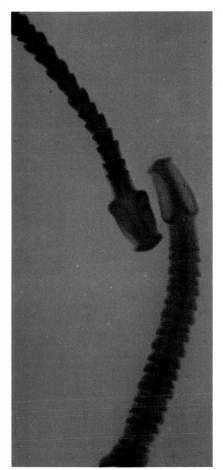

The tapeworm *Eubothrium salvelini*. Photo by L. Margolis.

COPEPODS

Copepods are crustaceans and some of them are fish parasites although many are quite harmless. Various species of *Argulus,* the fish louse, (sometimes classified separately from the copepods) are fairly large and should be removed with a pair of forceps, being around ¼". Sea horses are favorite hosts but any fish can house them. Remove any that are detected without delay, as eggs are soon laid in the tank and can result in an infestation that is very hard to cure chemically.

Visible signs of other copepods may be egg-sacs hanging from the fish, the rest

of the animal being beneath the skin. In other cases the whole creature may be seen hanging from the gills or body. Affected fishes show discomfort, sometimes dashing around the aquarium. The same in-tank treatments with DTHP as for *Benedenia* can be applied, but should be continued for a month to deal with persisting larval stages.

EXOPHTHALMOS (Pop-Eye)

This condition is a symptom rather than a disease and may accompany various diseased states. One or both eyes protrude from the sockets, sometimes proceeding to blindness or loss of the eye. When not caused by disease, it may be due to toxic conditions in the aquarium, to gas bubbles, or to copper poisoning. All of these should be considered, as treatment depends on the probable cause. Remove

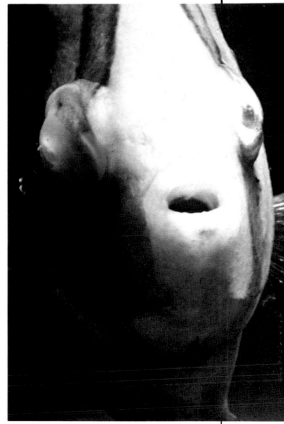

Although this butterflyfish obviously has a bad case of pop-eye, there is no way of diagnosing the cause or suggesting a reliable treatment without knowing more about its history and the history of the tank. Photo by Frickhinger.

Anchistrotos, a fairly normal appearing parasitic copepod from the gills of a boxfish. Many parasitic copepods are bizarre in shape and hard to recognize as crustaceans. Photo by Frickhinger.

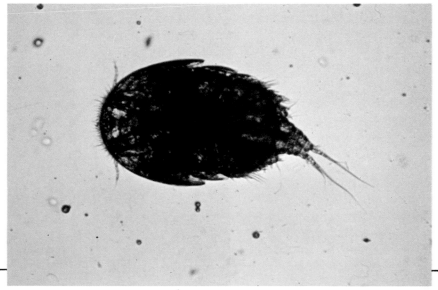

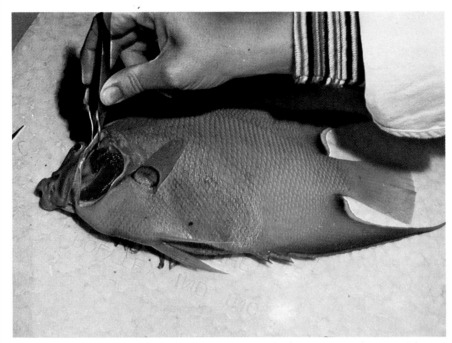 

Poisoning often appears suddenly and violently in the aquarium and is very hard to diagnose and even harder to treat. One of the first signs typically is unusual behavior, followed shortly by unusual color changes. The young Queen Angel at the right is exceptionally pale for the species, which could be a sign of extreme stress and perhaps some type of environmental poisoning. On autopsy the gills of a poisoned fish sometimes are exceedingly pale, constrasting greatly with the normal bright red gills of a healthy fish (left). In actuality, by the time you realize that you have a poisoning situation, it probably is too late to do anything effective about it. Photos by Dr. M. P. Dulin (left) and Dr. F. Yasuda (right).

copper with activated carbon, lower the temperature, and stop excess aeration if gas embolism seems probable. Clean up the tank thoroughly as well.

EXTERNAL POISONS

Various household materials can poison your fishes, especially ammonia-containing substances—cleaners, window sprays, kitten baskets, or animal cages in the same room. Insecticides can do it. So can many other household sprays, paints, cleaning agents, and bleaches based on chlorine compounds. Detergents on improperly rinsed hands or articles, tobacco or snuff can all be introduced by accident. Copper poisoning from make-up water is far from unknown. Never use water from a hot water system or metal storage tank or from copper pipes, old or new, without testing it for its copper content!

Whenever there appears to be no specific disease or parasites, but the fishes are behaving oddly, suspect one of the above. Any sluggishness, rapid respiration, going off food, color changes, dashing around the tank, or other unusual happening, should be investigated.

INTERNAL POISONS

The same symptoms can be due to malfunction within the tank; clogged filters, algae dying, overfeeding, a dead fish or invertebrate, overcrowding, can all cause the release of toxins. Ammonia, hydrogen sulphide, and phenols are the usual causes of trouble, with about that frequency of occurrence. Ammonia in the amounts concerned is odorless, but hydrogen sulphide smells of rotten eggs. It is generated when gravel or filters become foul and lack oxygen and is deadly at less than 1 ppm. The test for it is your nose. Phenols don't smell, but are released by some cheap plastics and by tubifex, decaying algae, or even some normal species of algae, and by some foods. Only a good once-over of the set-up and a good think will help you to decide the probable cause of trouble.

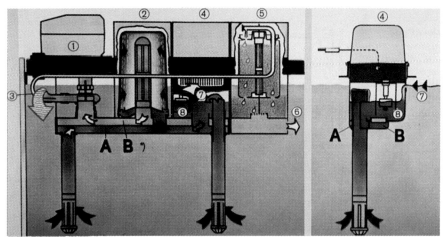

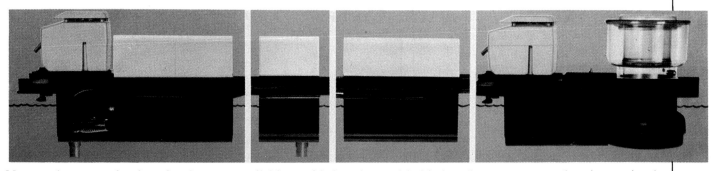

More and more technology has become available to aid the advanced hobbyist who wants more than just a simple display tank with a few common fishes and an invertebrate or two. Special filters, skimmers, pumps, lights, and other devices now allow the hobbyist to virtually duplicate marine environments in the home, with a sparkling tank and healthy fishes and invertebrates. Photos courtesy Tunze Systems, Sea Kleer Reefs, Inc.

Every marine aquarist has wished that he could turn his tank into a miniature version of a tropical reef, and now he can satisfy that desire. By carefully following the instructions in this book even the beginner, if willing to make an investment in time, patience, and money, can have a beautiful duplicate of the Great Barrier Reef or Jamaica. Art by J. R. Quinn.

Miniature Reef Aquaria

It has been the ambition of many an aquarist to keep invertebrates and fishes in a home aquarium that looks like a segment of a natural coral reef. This ambition has been brought to reality by some of our European friends, particularly the Germans and the Dutch. In fact, they keep "minireefs" that are more densely populated than the great majority of real reefs that rarely have more than 50-60% of live coral and are not as crowded with other creatures. Their techniques were slow to spread at first, but interest in them has flared up in many other countries during the past few years as it became apparent that they work. Miniature reef aquaria now come in many forms, but they all share certain essential characteristics that make them what they are.

Essentially, such a crowded aquarium must have a very efficient system for purifying the water. Even nitrates must be kept at a low level compared with an ordinary aquarium or corals and some other creatures will not flourish. Gas exchange must be at a maximum to keep the oxygen content high and to get rid of excess carbon dioxide. Lighting must be intense enough to keep the symbiotic algae of corals and anemones and others, such as giant clams, functioning, and it must have the necessary spectral characteristics for success. To achieve all this, we must modify our views on what

is needed in such a tank, or in operation with it. A coral reef has the vast ocean to back it up and gets continual changes of water that has been oxygenated by wave motion over most of its area, and we must do as much with the same aquarium water day after day.

External Biological Filtration

Efficient as the undergravel filter may be, it has two drawbacks. First, it is operated by aerobic bacteria that must consume oxygen to convert ammonia to nitrites and then to nitrates; second, it eventually clogs up and must be "renewed" in stages. You can't just haul it all out and start again because it is an essential part of the works. The Europeans never took to undergravel filtration with any enthusiasm, mainly for the second reason, and preferred to keep their biological filters external to the aquarium. This enabled them eventually to explore the advantages of an aerated biological filter, now known as the wet-dry (or dry-wet) filter. This external filter drips water from the aquarium at a fast rate over an exposed filter bed that is otherwise filled with air, sometimes just passively and sometimes with an airstone beneath it. The water may then pass over a further series of filters, biological or carbon, etc., and is eventually returned to the tank.

The earlier forms of wet-dry filter consisted of a sprinkler bar or bars fixed over the top of a series of trays of coral gravel,

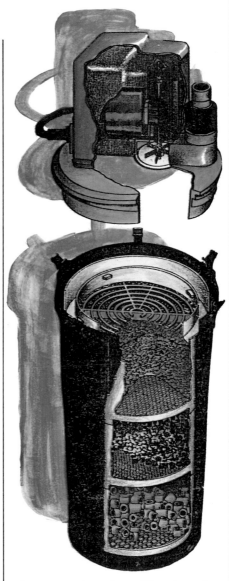

An external canister filter is satisfactory for simple marine aquaria but unsatisfactory for the miniature reef aquarium. It is basically a modification of the old external filters familiar to most aquarists, using various ceramic and charcoal substrates to act as a biological filter when properly primed and allowed to age for a proper period. Such filters are still excellent for normal aquaria but not as efficient as the newer wet-dry filters.

A "Dutch" miniature reef aquarium setup showing the four drip trays and other filters.

each quite shallow and with a perforated base allowing the water to flow down onto the next tray. The original "Dutch" minireef had four such trays. The last tray in the stack directed the water into a series of four compartments seated below it, the first two being conventional undergravel-type submerged filters of coral gravel, the third a carbon filter, and the fourth a pump compartment sending the water back into the tank. All this was placed in a cupboard below the aquarium and the water entering it was skimmed from the top of the tank via a "pre-filter" described below. A supposed advantage of continuing to use crushed coral in such a filter is that it helps to keep the water alkaline, but the extent to which this is true is debatable because of the pH of seawater and because of the coating of bacteria present.

Later forms of wet-dry filters have at least the coral in the "dry" section replaced with plastics. This may take the form of perforated plastic balls, such as the original Dupla bioballs, or of plastic matting, the most efficient of which seems to be the double spiral type placed on end with a rotating sprinkler above it. With such dry filters, there doesn't seem to be much for the wet part to do and it is omitted in some designs. An efficient filter of this type is reported to be three times as good as a submerged filter, and if it is conditioned by using ammonium salts this may well be exceeded. Any necessary heater is usually placed in the pump compartment, and due to heat losses from evaporation

Although complex marine aquaria (top) were occasionally operated as long as two decades ago, it has only been recently that the technology to maintain a modern miniature reef aquarium (bottom) was available to any interested hobbyist. Photos by P. Wilkens.

One of the secrets of the modern marine aquarium is the filter and the filter medium. Although the "Dutch" system required large amounts of space in which to operate, it was basically a biological filter operating somewhat along the manner of a sewage treatment facility. By using newer Space Age materials to produce remarkably complex bacterial substrates such as Bioballs and others, much of the workings of a tray filled with coral can now be condensed into a few pounds of plastic and ceramic balls and spirals.

One of a pair of ion exchange resin chambers used in assuring the proper water quality of a miniature reef aquarium. By careful choice of resins and correct circulation of the water, the most delicate chemistry of marine waters can be manipulated to the betterment of the animals.

Above: A hobbyist interested more in the scientific aspects of marine aquaria than strictly in a display aquarium can become very involved with the mechanics and technology of the hobby. Fortunately the average aquarist doesn't have to worry about such an unsightly setup.

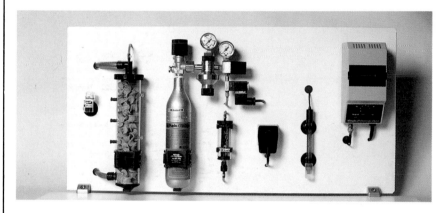

Below: Although many hobbyists may be satisfied with this jumble of pipes and tubes and canisters, this clutter is unnecessary as many of these seemingly random tubes, etc. can be "packaged" into much neater containers.

Above and center right: Carbon dioxide diffusion is now being used by the most advanced hobbyists in attempts to aid the growth of corals and other animals and plants that require unusual amounts of the gas to produce calcareous exoskeletons and other deposits. The gas is passed through a cylinder packed with oyster shell or other calcareous substrates (above). The release is carefully monitored and controlled electronically (right).

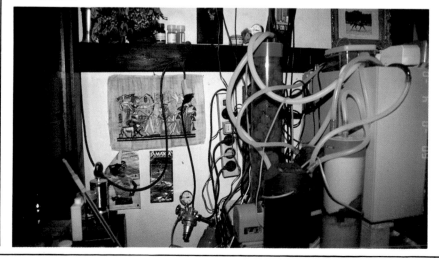

The tidy unit above contains cylinders of filter substrates such as bi-obeads and bioballs.

and external filtration, this should be 30-50% more powerful than the usual calculations would indicate. The advantages of the plastic filters are lightness and, in the case of the spiral ones, quietness.

Protein Skimming

Protein skimmers or foam fractionators are increasingly regarded as desirable in the reef aquarium and may be sited in the pump compartment or, for greatest efficiency, outside the rest of the filtration set-up. They remove organic matter that has not yet been reduced to ammonia and prevent the water from yellowing with age. In doing so they also reduce the burden on the biological filter. A skimmer inside the pump compartment must necessarily be rather short, whereas a long one is more efficient. For elegance, it can be placed behind the aquarium, if possible, otherwise it must sit beside it and reduce the attractiveness of the arrangement. Some enthusiasts use it intermittently and store it away when not in operation. A carbon filter does much the same job and can be more readily accommodated in the below-tank cabinet normally used, but the general opinion is that a protein skimmer is more effective. You can of course use both. I substituted polyfilters for a carbon filter in one large aquarium and find them very efficient although rather slow in bringing about changes in water quality.

Oxygenation

It is not desirable to include airstones in the reef aquarium because the top is not covered

Much of the equipment used in large freshwater aquaria can be adapted to smaller marine aquaria. The ultraviolet sterilizer above also will function with saltwater, while the small canister filter below can be used in groups for smaller or moderate marine aquaria.

by glass as in an ordinary tank and splashing or spraying onto lights, etc. must be kept to a minimum. The water returning to the tank may be injected via a sprinkler bar raised a little above the water level, but even this causes splashes and is best kept just under the surface rather than over it. It then creates a brisk downward flow, dragging surface water down with it and thus helps in oxygenation. It is also quiet. How then is a high degree of oxygenation maintained? It is done by leaving an open surface, agitated preferably by a small fan or airjet, or by an auxilliary pump or pumps directing a flow just under the surface of the water. Without these, a circulation rate of 5-6 tank volumes per hour is optimal, but with them a rate of around 3 volumes per hour is enough.

Oxygen uptake is also assisted by skimming off the surface water in one corner of the tank so that it is delivered to the filters below via a pre-filter built within the tank. This corner filter then discharges through a hole at the bottom sealed onto a plastic tube connected with the sprinklers of the wet-dry filter. It contains only plastic matting to remove any coarse materials that flow over from the aquarium. The arrangement has the advantage that the film of fatty and proteinaceous material that collects on the surface is constantly removed and this in collaboration with the agitation much enhances oxygen uptake. Carbon dioxide also flows down into the pre-filter instead of tending to accumulate over the water surface.

Further enhancement of

Above: Diatom and other particulate matter filters are handy for cleaning the water in the aquarium at regular intervals. They remove much suspended detritus.

oxygenation is contributed by the "dry" filter. Instead of using up oxygen as does an undergravel filter, it is so well aerated that little is removed and that is renewed as the water drips into the compartment below. The probably unnecessary wet filter if present, has so little to do, that it does not cause further depletion. A high degree of saturation is really needed, because sea water at 25°C (77°F) holds only 4.8 ml of oxygen per liter. Anything less than 3 ml per liter is insufficient both for sensitive sea creatures and for biological filtration to be effective; 4 ml per liter is the minimum desirable level. If a protein skimmer is in use, the oxygen level is still further enhanced by its vigorous mixing of air and water—or of ozone and water if the former is used.

Lighting

The reef tank requires very good lighting, mainly to service the algae that live inside corals, some anemones, and various other creatures. These will die off if not brightly illuminated,

Small motor-driven filters are useful with small marine setups and also to help pump water through larger filters and prefilters.

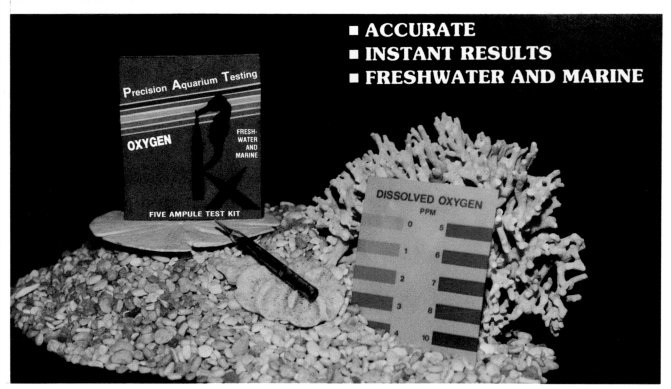

- **ACCURATE**
- **INSTANT RESULTS**
- **FRESHWATER AND MARINE**

Above: Because of the often extraordinary oxygen requirements of marine fishes and invertebrates, the hobbyist must always be aware of oxygen levels in the tank. Test kits are available at your local pet shop.

and that is achieved by two strategies—sufficient light of the right sort and placement of the inhabitants that need it in the near vicinity of the sources of light (unless these are very intense). There are only two sources that need be discussed, fluorescents and metal halides. Other types have proved unsatisfactory in the long run for one reason or another. Other algae vary in their light requirements, but none need as intense a light as the symbiotic zooxanthellae (yellow-brown algae) and zoochlorellae (green algae) of corals, etc., probably because much of it is absorbed by the tissues of the host before it gets to the algae inside them.

If you want to keep higher algae and corals, you will need the proper lights. Algae are of course photosynthetic, and corals rely on internal algae for nutrition and to help build their calcareous exoskeletons. Metal halide and other specialized miniature reef lights are widely available and must be used to keep specialized invertebrates successfully and produce fields of green and red seaweeds. Courtesy Energy Savers Unlimited, Inc.

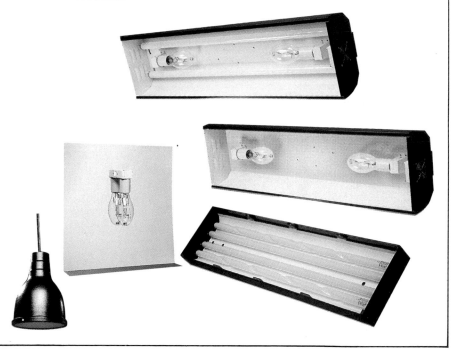

To successfully keep corals and even some anemones you need a higher intensity of light than can be provided by normal aquarium fixtures.

The average intensity of light, the flux, in daylight hours in the tropics is 50,000 lux, peaking at 100,000 lux at noon. However, much light is lost as we descend into the ocean, so much so that at 10 meters (33 feet) in clear conditions only 20% of the blue-green light and less than 3% of red light persists. Algae need both red and blue light, particularly the latter, although brown or red varieties can also utilize much of the intermediate spectrum because they carry pigments that absorb it and pass the energy on to chlorophyll. Green algae depend more strongly on the blue and red ends of the spectrum, hence the popularity of purple light from plant-stimulating fluorescents. These may not, however, produce as much light overall as ordinary daylight or white tubes and so the situation is complicated. The point to be made is that algae in general get along well at 10 meters depth. So do many corals that contain them, so that a flux of the right kind of light (predominantly blue) is what we must aim at providing, and it need not be as intense as tropical daylight.

John Burleson has perhaps done more experimenting with fluorescents than anyone else and his results fit nicely with the above discussion. He finds that the use of Actinic-03 fluorescents in combination with whites gives the best results. Actinic-03 tubes produce an intense blue light that stimulates algae to perform, but to our eyes they are rather dull-looking. The combination with normal tubes gives a pleasant appearance to the aquarium and sufficient light overall to promote the health and growth of both hermatypic (algae-containing) and ahermatypic (no algae) organisms. Too much ultraviolet light is detrimental to algae, which is probably why they do not grow as well near the surface of tropical seas as they do 20 or 30 feet (6-9 meters) down. Actinic-03 fluorescents produce no ultraviolet light. The number of tubes used depends on the size and depth of the aquarium. Typically, three tubes, one or two actinics with one or two daylight or white tubes, are needed over a 50-gallon (200 liter) tank and four over a 100-gallon (400 liter) tank. There will be a hood over them, but open at the back with a small fan or air supply keeping the top of the tank reasonably cool.

Metal halide lamps run hot and cannot be placed near the water surface. They also produce too much ultraviolet light and a sheet of glass is best placed between them and the water, but not so as to prevent good air exchange. They must be suspended a foot or more above the aquarium but give out so much light that this distance doesn't matter. They also should be provided with a good reflector. One 175 watt lamp is recommended per 2 ft (60 cm) of aquarium length. They provide a good imitation of natural daylight and give a very bright appearance to the aquarium - you can take photographs without flash or any additional lighting.

Denitrifying Filters

The end products of the nitrogen cycle, nitrates, accumulate in the normal aquarium unless they are removed by growing algae or massive water changes. There must be a lush growth of any kind of algae to remove sufficient nitrates, with the necessity of constant thinning out and regrowth, lusher than the average miniature reef possesses (although some do). Hermatypic corals and other algae-possessing organisms, if growing, will also mop up some nitrates as well, so that the accumulation in the reef aquarium is fairly slow, but even then it usually occurs. Corals and many other invertebrates do not do well in nitrate-rich water; around 15 ppm is about their limit. So if natural events and some water changes do not keep nitrates down, a denitrifying or "denitra" piece of equipment should be used.

A denitra filter utilizes anaerobic bacteria that flourish in the absence of oxygen. They convert the nitrates to gaseous

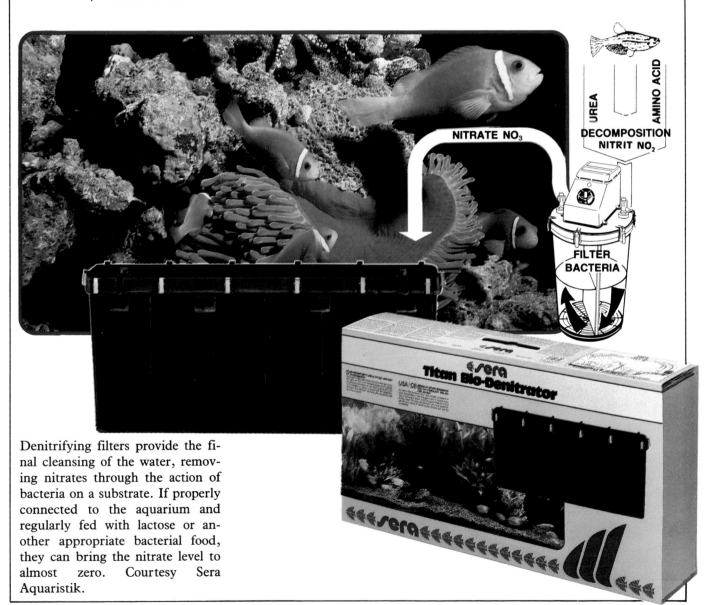

Denitrifying filters provide the final cleansing of the water, removing nitrates through the action of bacteria on a substrate. If properly connected to the aquarium and regularly fed with lactose or another appropriate bacterial food, they can bring the nitrate level to almost zero. Courtesy Sera Aquaristik.

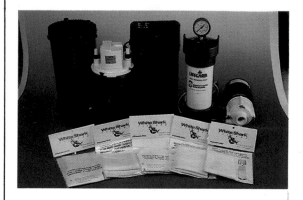

Specially treated and formed substrates for canister filters encourage the growth of the proper bacteria for biological filtration.

Canister filters (above and below) are packed with substrate materials designed to produce tremendous surface areas for bacterial filtering. Such filters work well with smaller tanks but cannot replace the advanced technology of wet-dry filters.

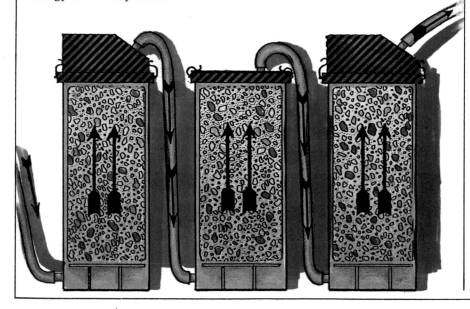

nitrogen that eventually passes out of the water, and can keep the nitrate level very low, even to virtually zero. This is a slow process and the denitra filter is usually fitted onto a bypass that bleeds off just a little of the water flowing to the aerobic filter and returns it to the main flow afterwards. The denitra filter needs a source of organic carbon to function, supplied as lactose or other simple compounds. These are fed regularly to the filter, which is composed of any suitable substrate for the bacteria to grow upon.

Living Rock

So much for the tank and its auxiliary equipment—now for what goes into it. Living rock is old dead coral, often compacted, that has been colonized by various invertebrates such as tubeworms, anemones, starfishes, small crustaceans, and molluscs. In addition, there will be algae or their spores and even small fishes. Many creatures not already mentioned in this book may appear and some will be difficult to classify. Different sources of living rock will provide very different populations, some of which will go on developing for months or even years. It all depends on how good it was to begin with and how it has been handled. Living rock is the basis onto which later additions will be built and the aquarium is filled with it from near top-back to near bottom-front—up to 2 lbs per gallon (1 kg per 4 liters) if you so desire.

To enjoy the plentitude of fresh living rock it must be transported from the ocean to

A small piece of living rock may contain dozens of species of coelenterates, sponges, and worms, plus a few crustaceans, mollusks, and even a sea squirt or two. Sponges also may encrust the surface and cracks of the rock. Many of these animals survive in the aquarium and eventually produce rich growths that not only look good but help condition the water. Art by J. R. Quinn.

your aquarium in the shortest time possible and keeping it moist the whole time. Then little will die off and the rock can be safely placed in the tank after the latter has been conditioned so that it is ready to deal with any breakdown products (some of which are inevitable). If possible, arrange a source of fresh rock that has not been placed in someone else's tanks prior to your getting it. If it was, some of the life will be lost, although perhaps only some of the free-living life such as shrimp and molluscs. When it arrives, pour the water present in as well for it is full of minute creatures. At the same time, get rid of any large crabs you detect as they are quite likely to feed

on too much of the other organisms present.

You may not be lucky enough to arrange for such a collection if you have to depend on rock from a dealer's tanks. This will vary in its nature, since it is often shipped dry and arrives largely dead, even having been purposely stripped of much life before being dispatched. The dealer then "cures" the rock (if necessary), leaving it in a tank provided with a biological filter until the dead material has been removed and the smell has abated. This results in a severely depleted specimen that has to revive gradually after being placed in the aquarium. It is surprising that anything redevelops, but it does.

Naturally, the full original population will not be seen again, but creatures will emerge from hiding, algae will spring up again, and a semblance of the original develops. Some aquarists actually prefer such rock as it will not contain dangerous inhabitants large enough to start trouble, although they can eventually develop from larvae still present.

It is not true, as is sometimes asserted, that the aquarium must be filled with living rock all at once. If you cannot arrange a large initial shipment, build up the rock gradually until it covers the back and much of the sides. In a large tank it is best to construct a base of cured dead

A properly filtered and conditioned tank with the proper high intensity lighting can, when filled with living rock, gradually become a beautiful display. From the barren rock (above), life gradually emerges and grows to produce a miniature reef background (bottom).

coral or stone so that precious living rock is not buried uselessly under other rock to any great extent. Leave plenty of spaces so that nocturnal creatures and sponges or other light-avoiding life can hide or develop there and where fishes can later take shelter. If the rock is built up all at once, make sure that you have fully conditioned the tank with ammonia or a commercial starter kit beforehand, or you will very likely end up with a malodorous soup. If it is built up gradually it is not normally necessary to do more than seed the filter with the necessary bacteria and it will then keep pace in development as more rock is added from time to time. Re-read the section on setting up to remind you of the steps to take.

Now is when you need patience. A tank filled right off with living rock must be left to settle down and the contents given a reasonable time to develop—just a few weeks with fresh living rock but up to a few months with previously dried rock that has to recover. However, it is astonishingly interesting to watch the progress of dried rock as little critters become visible and algae start to develop again from spores on the rock or in the water. After a few weeks you can add a few hardy invertebrates to add interest, but not yet corals or anything likely to be touchy. All additions must be gradual, as the biological filter only slowly adjusts to new levels of ammonia production or other pollutants. Even if it was fully conditioned before you started it will have fallen to whatever level is being demanded of it as the reef develops, and it never has a greater capacity than that until the demand arises and it slowly adjusts. Allow a week between additions for this reason and restrict them to one average sized specimen per 25 gallons (100 liters).

If you are building up the reef gradually, you can keep pace with the addition of invertebrates as well, still following the rule above, but with no corals at first either. Some macro-algae, such as *Caulerpa* can also be added if not already present on the rock. Preferably build the reef from one side of the tank across the middle to the other side, not from the bottom up or you will have to keep rearranging it. The dead cured coral recommended can of course be in position from the beginning. Keep an eye on the development of a tasteful arrangement with plenty of niches or platforms that will accommodate new specimens as they are acquired. Leave room for corals to be placed near the top—except for those that need less light, such as many soft corals or gorgonians. Don't forget, whichever method you use to build up the reef, to keep frequent checks on what is happening to the water—at least nitrite, nitrate, pH, and specific gravity should be measured every few days at first and weekly later on. Months later, occasional nitrate, pH, and specific gravity measurements should be enough unless something drastic has occurred.

Living Corals

For reasons that are not completely understood, living coral does not do well in a

Thanks to newly available algal cultures and actinic lighting, it is now possible to grow lush fields of complex seaweeds such as *Halimeda* (above) in the aquarium. Unfortunately seed coral colonies such as shown below are not yet available.

newly set-up reef aquarium. This is particularly true of hermatypic corals, but partially true of the ahermatypics as well. Try an ahermatypic coral or two a month or two after setting up, and if things go well, start to add others, plus some hermatypics, a little later. If the first introductions die off, wait a few weeks and try again. Place the ahermatypics in lower, shadier areas and the hermatypics toward the top where they will receive full illumination. Remember that sunlight comes in parallel rays and so loss of light occurs only because of cloudy water as depth increases. With artificial lighting the loss is much greater as depth increases, even in perfectly clear water, because the light is spreading out from bulbs or tubes and is not in parallel rays like sunlight. Reflections from the glass and adequate top reflectors can make a big difference, so don't think in terms of the inverse square law, but much light will still be lost. The shading created by some of the rockwork means that there will be some quite dark regions too, where creatures not liking much light can thrive.

Do not allow any coral or other organism to remain in the aquarium if it is obviously dying as it will foul the water and could start a wipe-out. This is particularly true in the early stages when there is little stability in the tank. Even later, it is unwise to leave dying or decaying material in the tank because even if nothing alarming results immediately you are helping to build up the nitrate content of the water and will have to make large water

Living corals must have sufficient light of the right intensities to support the symbiotic algae. Dead corals may serve as points of attachment for encrusting algae and may look attractive in the aquarium, but to an advanced hobbyist they are no substitute for living, growing coral. Photo of *Achrelia horrescens* by Dr. Herbert R. Axelrod.

changes to bring it down—unless you have a denitra filter in operation or very lush algal growth.

Algae

Reef aquaria vary widely in content and appearance. Some have luscious algal growth and may need no denitra filter, others are virtually bare of algae. In the early stages algae may not thrive, except for brown or red varieties, the former mostly diatoms. These may be a nuisance and need frequent removal but should eventually die off, after which green hair algae may then take their place and should be kept in check as well. What we want is fronded, higher algae that are decorative and help to keep the water pure. If introduced early they may only die off or get eaten by crabs, but persist in introducing them and they will eventually take over. Then, they must be cropped regularly to keep them in check and to remove the nitrates and other pollutants that will have been mopped up by them as they grow. Don't let decaying algae remain in the tank or they will return the materials you want them to remove.

The easiest algae to introduce, if not already on the living rock, are various *Caulerpa* species, of which there are many. They have the valuable property of growing from cuttings and do not need, as do most algae, to be introduced attached to a rock or other base by a holdfast—the algal equivalent of a root. They are green algae that come as simple fonds *(C. prolifera)*, fern-like *(C. mexicana, C. crassifolia,* etc.), with rounded grape-like

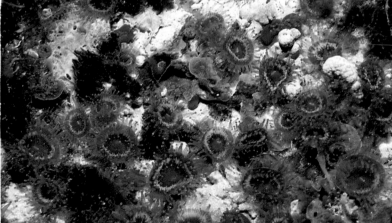

Ahermatypic corals tend to grow either too deep for light penetration or in caves and overhangs where there is little light, so they lack symbiotic algae and need lower light intensities than do reef-building (hermatypic) corals. These corals occur singly (bottom) or in small but sometimes dense colonies (top, *Tubastrea*) and can be quite colorful. Photos by R. Steene.

knobs *(C. racemosa, C. peltata),* cactus–like *(C. cupressoides)* or like a shaving brush *(C. verticillata),* and so on. So you have a nice choice of easily grown plants.

Other green algae, usually to be introduced somewhat later as they do not always thrive in a new tank, are mostly partially calcified and must be obtained with their holdfasts attached to something or they rarely do well. Some of the most popular are Neptune's shaving brush *(Penicillus* spp.), baby bows *(Halimeda discoidea)* with circular plates, sea fans *(Udotea* spp.) and sea lettuce *(Ulva* spp.) the last two looking as their names suggest. Brown and red algae are generally not very popular, brown algae because they are dull and often fall to bits, red algae because they tend to be encrusting or enveloping nuisances, although there are some attractive species. All algae undergo alternation of generations, meaning that a sexually produced generation alternates with one or more asexual ones that may or may not look like the sexual generation. So, apart from the caulerpas, do not expect to propagate them by cuttings or even to recognize the next generation should it happen to appear.

Water Quality

For the reef aquarium, certain characteristics of the water need to be kept within stricter limits than in other marine tanks if some of the invertebrates are to flourish. Hard corals in particular do not like departures from the properties of ordinary seawater. The pH, alkalinity, nitrate concentration, specific gravity, and temperature have their various limits beyond which there is danger. The pH should stay between 8.0 and 8.3 (best at 8.2), and when maintaining it with sodium bicarbonate carefully check the alkalinity as well. Alkalinity measures the buffer capacity of the water, and although it is not usually checked by marine aquarists, it pays to do so as hard corals do not react well to too high a level. Seawater has an alkalinity of 2.0 - 2.5 milliequivalents per liter (meq/l) or, as measured by the Germans, 5.6-7.0 DKH (degrees of carbonate hardness). Keep to a reading of 2.5 - 4.0 meq/l or 7.0-11.2 DKH. If the alkalinity rises above that range, don't panic, just let it fall again to within the range before adding any more bicarbonate. Measure pH and alkalinity two days after adding the bicarbonate since they do not settle down immediately.

Good marine salts are still an essential element of a successful marine aquarium.

Also needing high light intensities, although probably not as high as hermatypic corals, are the zooanthids (top), close relatives of the anemones. Some contain symbiotic algae similar to those of the corals. Complex marine algae (i.e., seaweeds) have varying light needs, but all need more light than produced by old-style aquarium fixtures. Healthy seaweed growth (bottom) is one sign of a healthy miniature reef tank. Photos by R. Steene.

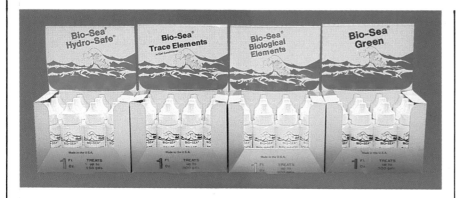

Sea salts are not just table salt with some other stuff added. Good sea salts are complex chemical mixtures of salts and trace elements in exacting percentages. The trace elements must be renewed regularly, and other additives to promote algal growth, etc. can be added as well.

Keep the nitrate concentration as low as you can, not letting it rise above 15 ppm if possible. A good denitra filter or plenty of growing algae will take care of the problem, but if you have neither water changes are necessary at a fairly high level. Here is where I shall get into hot water, no pun intended, because some miniature reef enthusiasts do not change any of the water and believe that to do so is dangerous. All I can say is that the experience of myself and friends is to the contrary as long as either natural sea water or a carefully prepared salt mix is used. This means checking your tap water before use, aerating after mixing, and checking pH, specific gravity, and temperature before adding it to the aquarium. Preferably, keep it for 24-48 hours before using it. All of its measured properties

except nitrate concentration should be very similar to those in the tank. Unless a rapid change is indicated because the nitrate has risen unduly, it is better to make frequent small changes than to make occasional large ones. Instead of 20% per month, make it 6% per week or even 1% per day, although there is no need to go to extremes. Why the increase in total changes when they are more frequent? Because the actual water replacement is less in those circumstances.

Maintain the true specific gravity near 1.025 or even just a little below it, say 1.024. This, with a hydrometer calibrated for 15°C (59°F), will read 1.021 to 1.022 at 78°-80°F. Fishes, as we have seen, can stand lower readings, but sensitive corals and other invertebrates cannot. Do not worry too much about temperature changes as long as

they are gradual. A reef aquarium can be maintained at anywhere between 76°-84°F, but to minimize evaporation it is best kept toward the lower end of that range. Evaporation in an open tank with wet-dry filtration can be quite high. To make up for it, add fresh water (not salt) to the pump compartment where it will be mixed with the tank water thoroughly before returning to the aquarium. Don't pour it over the filter or it may disturb the bacteria, or directly into the aquarium either.

With adequate water changes, there is no need to add trace elements or calcium, etc. to the aquarium, but if they are not made it is wise to do so. You can purchase trace elements and also vitamins with instructions for their use. Don't overdo things; probably half the recommended doses will be enough. Calcium can be added as the solid carbonate or sulphate in the base of the filter where, if needed, it may be taken up as the water passes over it. Although an alkaline solution like seawater won't dissolve calcium very easily, enough is apparently dissolved. You may notice that many artificial salts have more iron in solution than is natural. This is to encourage algal growth, so if you happen to be using ocean water, iron can be added to a concentration of not more than 0.1 ppm. Kits for doing this are available.

More about Corals

Look back over the invertebrate section to remind yourself of some of the invertebrates suitable for marine aquaria because I am now going to expand on it to discuss its relevance to reef aquaria.

You can keep hard corals in reef aquaria and even see some of them grow, but even so, not all of them will do well or be particularly suitable. What is mainly wanted for our enjoyment of such aquaria are so-called "day" corals, that open by day instead of opening by night, which is what most reef-building corals do.

It may seem strange that the reef-building corals should do this, as their symbiotic algae would seem to be disadvantaged, but that's how it is. The facts must be that sufficient light gets to the algae by day and by night the corals feed on the plankton that rise into the upper layers more at night than by day. Some corals open both day and night, but not many, and a few others look good in the aquarium even when closed.

The genus *Goniopora* offers day corals that are relatively tough, some even being found in cloudy water. They come in about 40 species, brown, green, gray, or near white in color, with 24 tentacled polyps on rounded or flattish heads. Like many corals, they are aggressive and will reach out to a surprising length to sting nearby corals, or other coelenterates. Care must therefore be taken as to where they are placed. The same species, by the way, can be of several different colors. The genus *Alveopora,* less aggressive but otherwise rather similar, offers a wider range of colors, including pink and blue or blue-gray. However, the majority of specimens of both genera are brown and you have to be very selective in order to obtain the more exotic colors. These colors are not well

exhibited until the coral is fully open, when what seemed to be a blue specimen may turn out to be brown. *Alveopora* species have 12 tentacles.

The genera *Euphyllia* and *Catalaphyllia* are also day corals, often referred to as meandering corals because their skeletons have circuitous channels in which quite large polyps with long tentacles live. They are connected with one another and like most corals form a community that feed one

Marine invertebrates also have special chemical needs that may not be supplied by the basic water. Extra calcium in a chemically available form is necessary for skeleton building in corals, for instance. Algae often need iron supplements, and of course sessile invertebrates need food that can be put directly into their mouths. All the essential supplements can be found at your pet shop.

Alveopora (above) and *Goniopora* (below) are relatively hardy corals that expand the polyps during the day. Both are rather aggressive and do not tolerate other corals nearby. Because they are hardy, they might make good hermatypic corals for the beginner. Photo above by D. Baker; that below by Takemura and Susuki.

another, if necessary, via these connections. *Catalaphyllia* has quite colorful green-striped polyp centers, with white or pink tips to the brown tentacles. Both genera do well in moderate light, but need a good current of water flowing over them. The genus *Favia* has some species with tiny polyps that spread over the surface of the rock and secrete quite colorful skeletons, although most are night feeders and close by day. I have a bright blue day species, probably *F. stelligera,* with both skeleton and polyps colored. Other types come in almost any color but are not plentiful.

Some of the night-opening corals are attractive by day because of the colors of their closed-up polyps which protrude from the skeleton. The grape or bubble corals, genus *Plerogyra,* are examples, so are the solitary corals *Cynarina* and *Fungia,* some of which show the same phenomenon. Other *Fungia* species open by day as well as at night. A single polyp may be six inches across with long waving tentacles, usually near white, brown, or green in color. The ahermatypic corals that live in dark areas offer further examples. The genera *Tubastrea, Dendrophyllia* and *Balanophyllia* are quite beautiful, with yellow, orange, and red or pink flesh when closed and usually yellow tentacles when open. Keep them in a shady area and they will open if food is offered—sometimes even when it is not. They must be fed, since they have no symbiotic algae to supply nutrients to them.

Soft corals have eight tentacles instead of the six or multiples of it possessed by the hard corals. Some are hermatypic but many are not. They have spicules of calcium carbonate and rarely form a hard skeleton, hence their name. However, *Heliopora* and *Tubipora* (organ pipe coral) have skeletons like a rather fragile hard coral and the gorgonians (sea fans) secrete a horny skeleton over which the polyps grow in a thick "rind". Ahermatypic soft corals are found in deep water, particularly the sea pens which are anchored in the mud by a special polyp. The remaining polyps are attached to a horny stalk, the rachis, and stick up into the water like a feather. Naturally, they are not particularly adapted to a miniature reef aquarium with its shallow sand, although they do well given a deeper substrate or if in a pot of some kind. Most soft corals available thrive in the aquarium if given the right conditions, but the very attractive *Dendronephthya* species, looking like colored trees with differently colored polyps, often do not. Try *Heliopora, Tubipora, Sarcophyton* and *Xenia* species, as they usually do well and are commonly available.

Gorgonians are hard to classify but are available in many shapes, sizes, and colors. Color is no clue to species, since as with most corals one species may come in a variety of hues. They need to be in a good current to prosper as they depend on collecting material from the water as it flows past them. They are found in cool as well as tropical waters but the cool water types, beautiful as they can be, rapidly die off in a tropical tank and must be

The delicate pinkish polyps of the coral *Galaxea fascicularis* from Guam are home to a small broken-rostrum shrimp, *Rhynchocinetes*. These shrimp have very large eyes and seem to be active mostly at night, when the coral polyps open up. Photo by D. Baker.

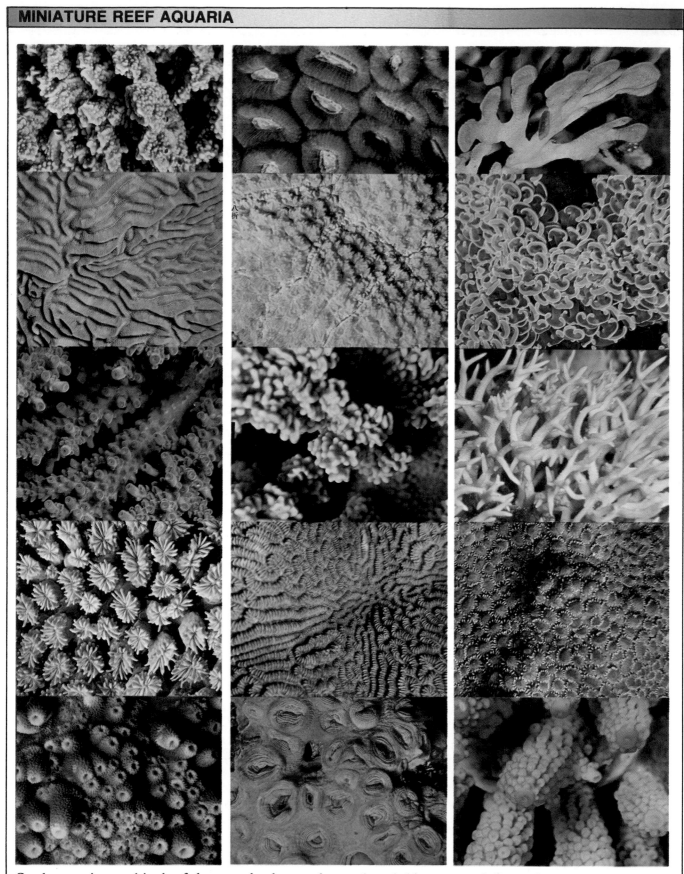

Corals come in a multitude of shapes and colors, and many have habits or growth forms that make them more or less suitable for the aquarium. Not all corals will survive in even the most advanced aquarium, and if you are wise you will discuss coral purchases with your dealer first. Photos by M. Goto, *Marine Life Documents*.

Some marine organisms presently cannot be kept in the aquarium because they simply will not adapt. These organisms are seen only by divers and photographers. Perhaps one day aquarium technology will be advanced enough to maintain red coral (*Corallium rubrum,* top) and the neon lantern sea squirt *Clavellina lapidaformis* (bottom).

avoided as they only pollute the water. They often open by day and come in so many forms that they must be seen to be believed. In the aquarium it is necessary to see that they are not clogged by algae. If it becomes a problem the presence of one or two algae-eating fishes that prefer hair or encrusting algae to *Caulerpa* etc. is a solution. The blennies, *Ecsenius bicolor* or *Salarias fasciatus,* or the surgeons, *Ctenochaetus* or *Zebrasoma flavescens,* are examples. These fishes are in fact a blessing in the aquarium, keeping hair algae in trim everywhere but not harming the fronded higher forms as do many of their relatives.

Corallimorphs

These attractive coelenterates have been relatively neglected both by zoologists and aquarists, the latter until recently, when the corallimorphs have become popular—as they should be. They are highly variable relatives of the corals with no hard skeleton and often without long tentacles. They colonize rocky surfaces but are not connected like coral polyps, often looking like anemones but distinguishable from them anatomically. When they arrive for sale at the pet shop it is hard to imagine how nice they can be. They are usually contracted up to next to nothing but in the

Euphyllia is a coral that has a distinctively shaped skeleton visible when the polyps are withdrawn. Most corals are identifiable for certainty only from details of the skeleton. Photo by M. Goto, *Marine Life Documents*.

aquarium they will gradually expand and grow, some to discs six inches or more in diameter. These are the "leather" corals *(Actinodiscus)* with little knobs instead of tentacles covering the disc and surrounding a central mouth.

Right: The corallimorph *Ricordea florida* from the Caribbean usually occurs as encrusting colonies that can cover large areas. They usually need fairly intense light. Photo by Dr. P. Colin.

Actinodiscus is often called the leather or mushroom coral because of its color and shape, but it is actually a corallimorph, a close relative of the sea anemones. Photo by Dr. Herbert R. Axelrod.

The full-blown glory of the coral reef with its literally hundreds of species of invertebrates and fishes may be imitated in the aquarium but never duplicated. Photo by M. Goto, *Marine Life Documents*.

They come in almost any color, plain or patterned, that you care to imagine. At night, they contract once more to little better than when they first arrived. From the seas around southern North America, look out for the genera *Rhodactis, Ricordea,* and *Corynactis.* Many corallimorphs carry algae and need plenty of light.

Zoanthids

These colonial anemone-like coelenterates also cover rocks or dead coral and are distinguishable from anemones by having a single row of tentacles along the edge of their disc. Some have symbiotic algae, others do not. They are usually quite small and do not offer the variety of shapes and colors of the corallimorphs, being normally brown and green, but they can look very attractive. Cerianthids have already been mentioned as best left out of the aquarium, reef or otherwise, as they are too lethal to small invertebrates or fishes.

Associations between coelenterates and arthropods are common. Some crabs and shrimp, like some relatives of the porcelain crab already mentioned, live on the larger anemones and rarely leave them. Coral shrimps, such as *Rhynchocinetes,* live with corals in a similar manner. Crabs not infrequently make use of anemones or other coelenterates in various ways.

The following photos serve to give an idea of the diversity of life on the reefs of the tropical Indo-Pacific. Photos by R. Steene.

Sponge clusters.

The starfish *Petricia vernicina* (above).

The brittlestar *Astrobrachion* on a gorgonian (below).

Goblet sponges.

A scarlet finger sponge (above).

A crinoid feeding while anchored on a sea whip (below).

Some decorate themselves with them, such as *Polydectus,* others hold them in their claws and actually fish with them for small prey or debris or use them in defense. Wierdest of all, some hermit crabs of quite different species cover themselves with anemones or zoanthids that eventually dissolve away the shell and become the crab's only protection. At least he doesn't have to search for any more shells!

Shrimps and Copepods

Some of the shrimps already mentioned in the invertebrate section live for quite some time, but many others have short lifetimes of around half a year, so do not expect too much from them. Nevertheless, they are popular and fairly cheap and well worth keeping. Really small ones will crop up from living rock, but don't last for long if there are fishes present. Copepods, although readily eaten by many fishes, are so prolific that they may continue to flourish in the aquarium and be a constant source of nourishment to the other organisms. Many are fish parasites, as we have seen, but they will not usually emerge from living rock, only from fishes carrying them when introduced into the tank. However, there are copepods that are parasites of a great variety of invertebrates and you are very likely to acquire some of them, but on the whole they seem to do little harm. They are found in or on molluscs, worms of various types, echinoderms, sea squirts, and sponges. The sponges are hosts to vast numbers of creatures that live in their intricate system of canals.

A dorid nudibranch.

A spindle cowry, *Volva*.

Hymenocerus picta.

Rock lobsters, *Panulirus cygnus*.

Octopus sp.

Thor amboinensis.

Tubularia, a hydroid.

Large heads of coral are common in natural habitats but seldom develop in the aquarium. Note that the living polyps are restricted to the top of the head in this coral. Photo by Dr. Herbert R. Axelrod.

Shrimps to look out for are the colorful species of *Periclimenes,* of which there is a fair selection. Mentioned earlier as anemone shrimp, other members of the genus live on various invertebrates such as sea urchins, sea cucumbers, and nudibranchs, and yet others are cleaners. Of the free-living cleaners, *P. yucatanicus* and *P. pedersoni* are common and decorative. The anemone shrimp, *P. brevicarpalis,* has quite colorful females but almost colorless males, so at least you know when you have a pair. There are also several species of *Stenopus* now available, most as worth having as *S. hispidus* and they are also cleaners. The ghost cleaner, *S. pyrsonotus,* is a greyish shrimp with a dorsal red stripe rather suggestive of a *Lysmata* species. Snapping shrimp or pistol prawns, whether decorative or not, are liable to give the uninitiated aquarist a severe shock, as their ability to produce a sudden loud noise very suggestive of glass cracking is to say the least disconcerting. They belong to the genera *Alpheus* and *Synalpheus,* some of which live in association with gobies. The shrimp digs a burrow and both shrimp and goby live in it. The large claws can help defend the fish and the shrimp from predators.

The genus *Rhynchocinetes* is remarkable in having a hinged rostrum (the spike on the top of the head). As they are colorful, (usually red) and live at peace with one another, they are aquarium favorites, although some species are nocturnal. Another colorful genus is the bumble bee shrimp,

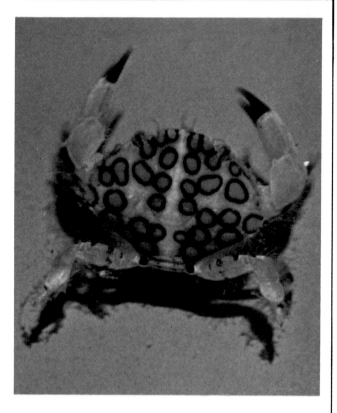

Colorful crustaceans. Above: A *Cycloxanthops* sp. mud crab from Baja California. Photo by A. Kerstitch. Left: *Lysmata grabhami*, the scarlet lady. Photo by B. Kahl. Below: *Uca vocans*, a fiddler crab. Photo by U. E. Friese.

Gnathophyllum, named after *G. americanus*, which does indeed look like a bumble bee. It would be nice to be able to get some of the deep sea shrimp that are characteristically red all over. They look black and hence invisible at medium depths where no red light penetrates.

Polychaete Worms

On the subject of color, the polychaetes are a puzzle. Think of a worm like *Spirographis*, stuck in its tube unable to move around, and yet it may be any color—red, blue, white, shades of brown, plain or speckled, and so on. Colors in fishes are thought to be for specific purposes—to camouflage them, for recognition of each other, or as a warning in some instances. What significance has color in *Spirographis*? It can't be for any of the purposes above and the fact that worms of different colors are found all together on

Above: A hermit crab, *Calcinus latens*. Photo by S. Johnson. Below: A large sabellid worm withdrawing into its tube as a tang passes nearby.

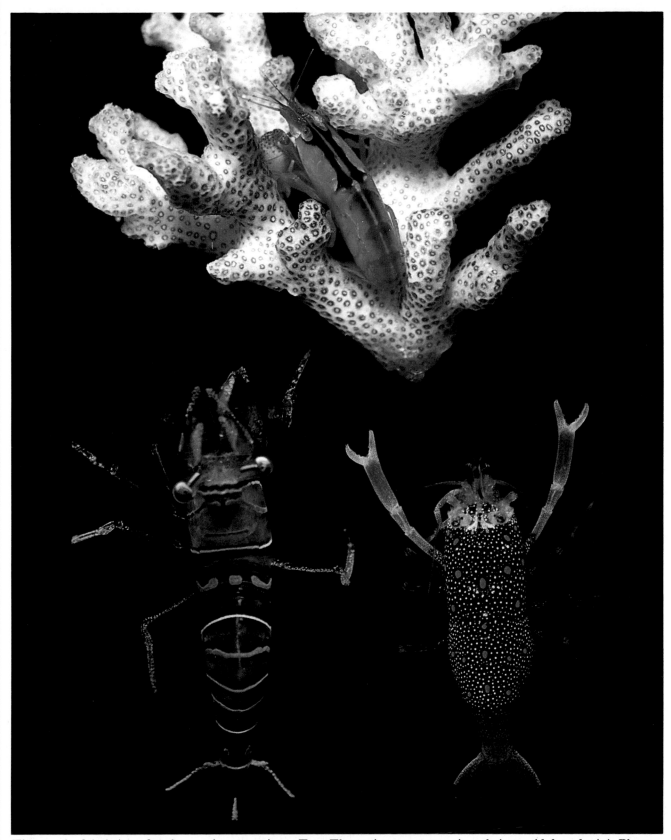

Three colorful shrimp for the marine aquarium. Top: The seriatopora snapping shrimp, *Alpheus lottiui*. Photo by U. E. Friese. Lower left: *Lebbeus grandimanus* from the cooler eastern Pacific. Photo by Dr. T. E. Thompson. Lower right: The Baja bumblebee shrimp, *Gnathophyllum panamense*. Photo by A. Kerstitch.

the same piece of coral suggests that color has no function. The same could be said of the leather corals that exhibit just the same phenomenon, as also do many hard corals and gorgonians, although in the last two cases the variety of colors is more restricted. It seems to be a peculiarly marine phenomenon since such color variation is rarely seen in land animals unless under domestication.

I have just been watching a female moon wrasse (*Thalassoma lunare*) in an aquarium containing some small *Spirographis* worms. Out of an array of about two dozen, she chose one particular blue worm and attacked it. Although it was retracted and behind its operculum (the lid that closes the tube), she persisted for ten of fifteen minutes until she got it out. She didn't show interest in any of the other worms before or after. Why that particular one? She was put in the tank to clean up some unwanted crabs, which she didn't do, and now I can't get her out without wrecking the whole set-up. It illustrates how careful you must be about what you put into a reef aquarium, especially in the way of fishes.

Other polychaetes than the ones mentioned earlier tend to be disappointing because you may rarely see them after

This exceptionally colorful mass of living rock is heavily colonized by beautiful serpulids. These worms present an amazing degree of color variation from one animal to the next, and even the two "arms" may differ in color. Photo by R. Steene.

Serpulids build calcareous tubes that are stoppered with ornamented opercula like the opercula of snails. First the arms are withdrawn, then the operculum. Photo by Dr. G. R. Allen.

putting them in the aquarium. The terebellid worms, although quite colorful, live in tubes and are not seen because they fish for food by means of long stringy tentacles. These spread out for long distances and have a coating of mucus. They also have cilia that propel material sticking to the mucus toward the mouth. You will see the fishing lines, but never the worm. The quite large burrowing scale worms (sea mice, *Aphrodita*) inhabit both warm and cold seas. When cleared of the

sand, etc. usually adhering to them, they are quite beautiful, but again they are rarely visible in the aquarium. You will have a selection of polychaetes like these, usually small species, that will equally rarely be seen except sometimes at night. Many of them are eaten by fishes when they can get at them, but in the aquarium they often survive unnoticed and may even reproduce. Various polychaetes burrow into coral although exactly how they do it is not clear.

Vermetid Snails, etc.

Not all the fishing lines you see in the tank are from terebellid worms. Some very similar ones come from the tube-building snails that immobilize themselves by converting their shells into tubes. Then they have to fish like any other fixed creature, which in some species they do by mucus-coated threads and in others by modified gills that fish in the water. What advantage they ever got out of this line of evolution is difficult to imagine,

This large tiger cowry, *Cypraea tigris*, would make an excellent addition to the aquarium. The mantle covers almost all the shell when the snail is actively moving around, making for very good camouflage. Photo by J. Deas.

but there must have been one.

Univalve molluscs will no doubt emerge from your living rock and may need watching, not only for the predaceous whelks and cone shells, but for the types that eat coral and other wanted coelenterates. The coral *Tubastrea* is attacked by snails and nudibranchs, for example, that consume either the polyps or the whole connecting tissues as well, leaving a bare white skeleton. Others will consume sponges, worms, and especially *Caulerpa*. One unidentified slug, green in color, looks so like part of the species *C. racemosa* that you only realize it is there when all you have left are slugs and bare stalks, if that much. Most nudibranchs that may crop up have a lean time of it because they are such specialized feeders, but occasionally they strike it lucky and find a feast awaiting them, much to your likely disgust. It doesn't pay to try to keep them for that reason—either they starve or decide to eat some precious specimen that is hard to replace. Even the popular cowries may prove to be pests and the more we learn about them the more we realize how specialized many species are in their diets.

The tiger cowrie, *Cypraea tigris,* is a vegetarian. So is the money cowrie, *C. moneta,* but their cousins the egg cowries and spindle cowries—the latter so-called because of their length—are on special diets. The white egg cowrie, *Ovula ovum,* seems to feed only on the soft coral *Sarcophyton,* while each species of spindle cowrie is found on and appears only to feed on a particular species of gorgonian, on which it also lays its eggs. One very useful specialized feeder that is a bit large for the home aquarium, as indeed is also its prey, is the triton, *Charonia tritonis.* It feeds on the crown-of-thorns starfish, *Acanthaster plancii,* and other stars. The crown-of-thorns starfish has, as you probably recall, proved a great destroyer of many Pacific Ocean reefs including parts of the Barrier Reef of Australia and controlling it has so far proved impossible.

Selecting Echinoderms

As with the molluscs, just which echinoderms to place in a reef aquarium depends in part at least on what else is there and in part on their particular habits. Some starfishes are persistent destroyers of algae, bryozoans, and other animals that coat living rock and give it such an attractive appearance, while others do not touch it. Even individuals within a species can differ in their habits. For example, the popular blue star, *Linkia laevigata,* is usually reported as "living on nothing", although it lives on satisfactorily. One aquarist had a specimen that cleaned up his living rock overnight. "Chunky" stars are not often good aquarium inmates and tend to foul the water; long-armed stars are usually safe even if not provided with bivalve molluscs to open, and will live on pieces of clam or other meat. Short-armed stars, like the biscuit star, *Patiria,* are most often algae or debris feeders and no nuisance in the tank. Feather stars are fine if you don't keep fishes that will peck at them or large crustaceans that will do the same. The algae eaters mentioned in connection with gorgonians are examples of fishes that would not harm them.

The blue starfish *Linckia laevigata* sometimes adapts to aquaria, but when it does the colors often darken. Photo by Dr. Herbert R. Axelrod.

Patiria miniata is a colorful small starfish whose broadly webbed arms product a graceful gliding effect when they move. Like most typical starfishes, they adapt well to pieces of fish and seafood but will prey on small mollusks and fishes in the aquarium. Photo by Dr. Herbert R. Axelrod.

Above: One of the few really attractive and keepable sea cucumbers, *Pseudocolochirus axiologus* from the Pacific Ocean. Photo by R. Steene. Below: *Pentagonaster* is a heavily plated and beautifully colored starfish.

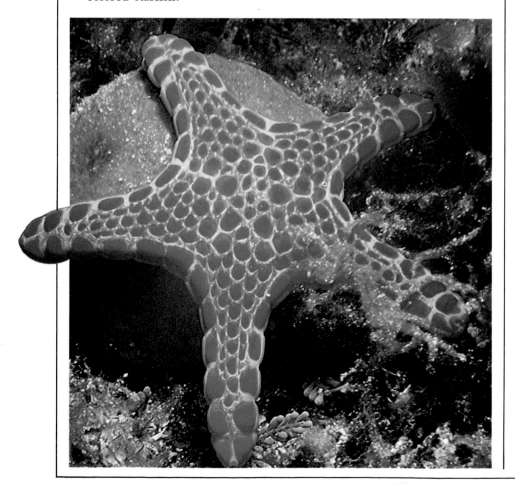

Most sea urchins are debris feeders and pretty omnivorous, eating dead animal material but rarely attacking live animals except small encrusting forms. They have powerful mouthparts, however, so any particular specimen should be watched to check that it does not turn out to be a rogue. They are generally immune from attack themselves in a reef tank, as you are most unlikey to be keeping fishes that could prey on them, such as triggers or parrotfishes, since these would be devastating the tank. Sea cucumbers are either debris or plankton feeders and safe for the aquarium except for their habit of emitting toxins or even much of their gut (which they regenerate) when seriously disturbed. A dead sea cucumber is also a menace since it poisons the water in a similar manner. Yet they are useful scavengers and some are decorative, so many an aquarist chooses to take the risk—its up to you, but realize that one dead sea apple, *Pseudocolochirus axiologus,* can wipe out a costly tankful of creatures. The sea apple is a member of the colorful plankton-eating order Dendrochirotida.

Moss Animals and Lamp Shells

The Bryozoa or moss animals, mentioned above, are mostly very small but form large colonies. They feed by means of a special organ, the lophophore, that distinguishes their phylum and a few other small phyla from the rest of the animal kingdom. The lophophore is a circlet of ciliated tentacles used in filter feeding. They secrete an exoskeleton of

Moss animals or bryozoans, such as the *Bugula neritina* above, sometimes enter the aquarium with living rock or shells.

Haliclona rubens is an attractive encrusting sponge that also may enter the aquarium on shells or rock. Photo above by K. Lucas, Steinhart Aquarium; that below by Dr. P. Colin.

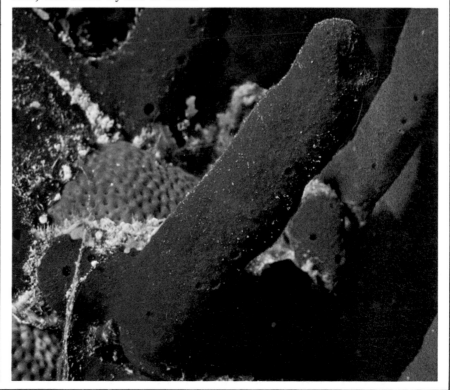

chitin plus lime in most cases, but there are exceptions, such as *Bugula,* which is soft and looks like a brown seaweed. They come in many forms and colors and make interesting additions to the reef tank, where they act as hosts to many small creatures and are unfortunately liable to be eaten by others.

Lamp shells, or brachiopods, having a hinged calcareous shell are easily mistaken for bivalve molluscs. However, internally they are quite different and they feed by means of a lopophore like the bryozoans. They attach to rock or coral like a mussel, although there are a few free-living species that burrow in the sand. You won't usually know if you have a lamp shell because of its strong resemblance to a bivalve mollusc, unless a fringe that

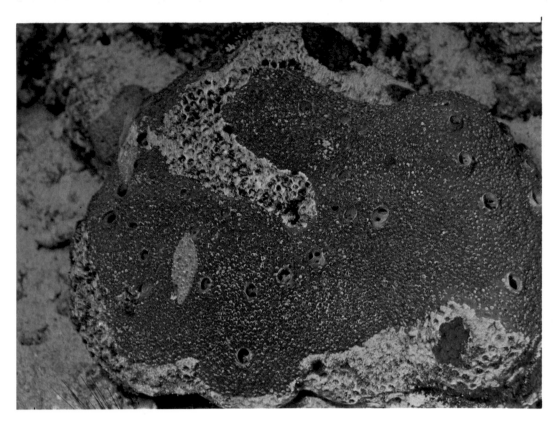

Although some sponges, such as this encrusting colony of *Cliona delitrix*, are attractive, they are dangerous in the aquarium as they are delicate filter feeders that may die without notice. Photo by Dr. P. Colin.

sometimes extends from the lophophore gives it away. If you do recognize it, salute, because you are looking at a very ancient phylum, members of which look much today as they did half a billion years ago.

Sponges

Another ancient phylum, the Porifera or sponges, do variably well in the aquarium, but have a better chance in the reef aquarium than in others because you will always be catering to the filter feeders. They often spring up spontaneously, grow for a period, and as often as not die off again. While in existence, their masses of tunnels make them an ideal home for a host of other animals. There are calcareous (with spicules of

calcium carbonate), siliceous (with spicules of silica), and spongin-containing sponges, that may have silica spicules as well. The simple, calcareous, or silicous sponges, often encrusting on rock, shells, or coral, are the ones you are likely to encounter and they come in all colors. *Cliona* species are usually red or yellow, *Haliclona* violet, *Hymeniacidon* orange, and so on. The glass sponges, forming delicate skeletons like the well-know Venus flower basket, come only from deep waters.

Sea Squirts

These are the creatures that spray you with water at low tide when you tread on them. They don't look like much, but be respectful because they are in

the same phylum, Chordata, as you are. Their larvae possess a notochord, but the adult is a sac with an inhalent and an exhalent syphon—another filter feeder. The notochord of the larva gives away its relationship to ourselves, for it is a primitive precursor of the backbone of vertebrates. The sea squirts, or ascidians, are an odd offshoot of the chordate line of development with no mobility once they have settled down. Many species are uninviting to look at, but some are nicely colored and look decorative in the tank, but unless well fed they usually fade away gradually. Some, like *Pyura* or *Ciona,* are solitary, others share the same outer covering and so form colonies on rocks, etc.

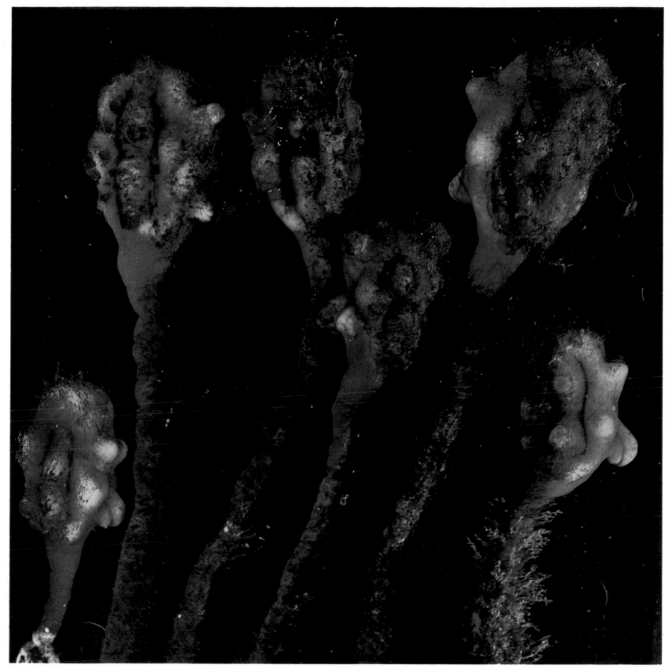

Although their bizarre form might tempt the hobbyist to add them to the aquarium, large sea squirts such as these sea tulips, *Pyura pachydermatira*, often spell trouble. There is always the possibility of a die-off contaminating the tank. Photo by K. Gillett, *Australian Seashores in Colour*.

Although not colorful, the sea squirt *Ciona* has an unusual shape. Most species come from relatively cool waters.

Fishes

As already noted, you have to be selective in adding fishes to the reef aquarium or they can wreck the whole set-up. Obviously, we don't want fishes that eat coral, too much algae, or small crustaceans if we intend to keep them. This means none of the usual surgeons, large angels, chaetodons, triggers, or many species of wrasse. Surgeons, with the exceptions already mentioned, eat all kinds of algae, angels eat variously algae, coral, sponges, and even shrimp. Chaetodons eat coral and much of what lives in it, triggers eat practically any meaty food they can get at, including even sea urchins, and wrasses in general love crustaceans.

It is best not to introduce many fishes early on—perhaps one or two hair algae eaters to keep it in trim, but no more. After a few months the collection can be built up to around one 2″ fish per 10 gallons. Too many fishes will cause problems—pollution, predation, and loss of other creatures. Start them small and by not overfeeding keep them that way. A reef aquarium produces food of its own. Even with its peculiar filtration there will still be some plant and animal plankton, including bursts of larvae of one kind or another, various sessile algae, and tidbits of various sorts, in the living rock. So keep feeding down to as much live or frozen food as possible, given sparingly only a few times a week. This is of course independent of the feeding of filter feeders, also to be given at about the same frequency. The

Cardinalfishes for the miniature reef aquarium. Top to bottom: *Apogon robustus*, *Apogon cooki*, and *Apogon fraenatus*. Because they tend to feed only on small food and ignore larger shrimp and the decorations, cardinalfishes do little to disturb the ecology of the reef tank.

If you do everything right, your tank will look like this. Photo by G. Smit.

Anemonefishes are good additions to the reef aquarium, especially if you can provide them with their anemones. From top to bottom: *Premnas biaculeatus, Amphiprion leucokranos,* and *Amphiprion latezonatus.*

fishes will take some of this as well, but most of it should be too small to interest them. Commercial invertebrate foods are aimed at the filter feeders and offer very fine suspensions best given with the main filter turned off for an hour or so and with an auxiliary pump keeping the water circulating. As an illustration of the thriftiness of fishes, I know of a pair of anemonefishes *(Premnas biaculeatus)* that are fed only twice a week and yet spawn regularly in their miniature reef tank.

Our restrictions on the types of fishes that can be kept in reef aquaria leave plenty still available. These include all of the anemonefishes and most of the damsels, some of which are good algae eaters, but not of the fronded types. Small wrasses such as cleaners *(Labroides dimidiatus), Coris* species, and small angels such as *Centropyge* species, as long as lush algae are present, are all acceptable. Cardinalfishes active by day, such as *Apogon orbicularis* and almost any small gobies and blennies do fine. Especially to be recommended are the firefish, *Nemateleotris magnificus,* the neon goby, *Gobiosoma oceanops,* and various blennies of the genera *Ecsenius, Meiacanthus,* and *Salarias.* The surgeons *Ctenochaetus* and *Zebrasoma flavescens* are safe and help to clean up hair algae while leaving most others alone. Dottybacks (Pseudochromidae) are a bit aggressive but nice to have, so are small serranids such as *Anthias* and *Hypoplectrus* species. The basslets, *Gramma* spp, are also elegant, but do tend to hide.

High hats, genera *Equetus* and *Eques,* and longfins, *Calloplesiops altivelis* or *C. argus,* make spectacular additions also.

You can also keep a tank with quite different fishes that would go poorly with practically all of the above. I am thinking of seahorses, pipefishes, and other slow feeders such as the dragonets or mandarins, *Synchiropus* species. A mixture of these fishes looks very attractive but they must be fed mainly on live food, although seahorses will take frozen mysid shrimp and the dragonets will eat frozen brine shrimp as well. They can even be kept with one or two small predators that do not eat the tiny foods that interest the slow feeders but will also leave the slow feeders alone, being too small to swallow them. Any young specimens of the Scorpaenidae (lionfishes), larger Serranidae (groupers), or Antennariidae (anglerfishes) would do. You would have to omit most shrimps from such a tank, but none of the above would do much harm to the general run of inhabitants.

DISEASES

Although it is wise to quarantine all incoming fishes, problems of disease in the reef aquarium are minimal. Some authors actually state that the aquarium has antibiotic or other curative properties, but that is going a bit too far. The likelihood is that the abundance of filter-feeders together with plenty of room for the fishes keeps parasites and even bacteria down to a minimum. The fishes should also be particularly healthy in the conditions of a super-aerated

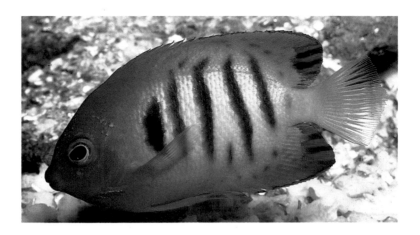

Although most angelfishes are too dangerous to put in the reef aquarium, feeding on living corals and the animals associated with them, the dwarf angels can sometimes be safely kept. From top to bottom: *Centropyge loriculus, Centropyge nox,* and *Centropyge heraldi.*

315

Because wrasses are avid eaters of crustaceans and often will rearrange the substrate looking for small shrimp and crabs, wrasses are not greatly favored in the miniature reef aquarium. Small *Coris* might be given a try, however. From top to bottom: *Coris gaimard africana, Coris formosa,* and *Coris formosa.*

tank and thus best able to withstand any attacks. Anyway, the good news is that disease in the miniature reef aquarium is rarely a problem and fishes already diseased tend to get over it when placed therein. This is lucky, because if disease or parasitism does happen to strike, you can't do much about it unless you can remove the affected fishes and you usually can't. The best advice is to ignore any mild attack of diseases like white spot or velvet, even of fin or tail rot or body streaks; they will probably disappear. I have never tried to treat disease in natural system or reef tanks and only once had a semi-wipeout and that was by purposeful neglect, when I let things go because I intended to clean the tank out anyway.

It would probably be safe to treat bacterial diseases by the administration of antibiotics in the food, but only in the food. Otherwise, filters would be affected and, for all I know so would some of the invertebrates. I very much doubt if any other treatment, for example those recommended for protozoal diseases, would be tolerated, except increased temperature, safe up to about 30°C (86°F) or a little higher if things appear tolerable. It must be remembered that the aquarium has a heavy load of sensitive invertebrates and a hard-working biological filter, and that both must be kept healthy. Almost all disease treatments are liable to hit one or the other or both.

Index

Page numbers set in **bold** type refer to illustrations

Index

Suggested Reading

DR. BURGESS'S ATLAS OF MARINE AQUARIUM FISHES
By Dr. Warren E. Burgess, Dr. Herbert R. Axelrod, Raymond E. Hunziker III
H-1100; ISBN 0-86622-896-9
This book contains over 4000 full-color photos, more than any other marine aquarium book ever published. It shows in full color not only the popular aquarium fishes but also the oddballs and weirdos, the large seaquarium type fishes, both warmwater and coldwater species. In short, this book has it all, and it has it in a format that provides maximum utility to readers. The book supplies the most up-to-date scientific names, and the captions indicate the family, range, size, and optimum aquarium conditions as well. Also included are family by family write-ups on the aquarium care of these fishes.
Hard cover, 8½ × 11", 736 pages
Contains over 4000 full-color photos

SALTWATER AQUARIUM FISHES
New Edition
By Dr. Herbert R. Axelrod and Dr. Warren E. Burgess
H-914; ISBN 0-86622-399-8

A very complete book, for the medium-level aquarist who has one or two saltwater tanks and wants to know the best fishes to keep and the best techniques for keeping them. This book has gone through a number of revisions and each edition brings many changes. Modern and up-to-date, and very popular with beginning and medium-level marine aquarists. Written on a high school level, the text covers the fishes on a family-by-family basis for the convenience of readers. A full chapter is devoted to the coverage of fascinating marine invertebrates. Contains over 400 full-color photos.
Hard cover, 5½ × 8½", 288 pages
Now revised so that every photo in the book (more than 400) is a full-color photo.

EXOTIC MARINE FISHES
By Dr. Herbert R. Axelrod, Dr. Warren E. Burgess, and Dr. Cliff W. Emmens
H-938L; ISBN 0-87666-103-7 (Looseleaf)
H-938; ISBN 0-87666-103-7 (Hardbound, non-looseleaf)

For the avid marine aquarist who has one or more tanks in his home. Covers setup and maintenance of saltwater tanks, but the main thrust of the book is its catalog of fish species, describing (and showing in full color) hundreds of species. Complete and authoritative; if the aquarist wants only one book on the subject, this is it. High school level.
Hard cover and looseleaf, 5½ × 8½", 608 pages
88 black and white photos, 477 color photos

THE ENCYCLOPEDIA OF MARINE INVERTEBRATES
By a panel of experts, each specializing in individual phyla
H-951; ISBN 0-87666-495-8
This excellent and enormously colorful book ranges widely over the invertebrate field and provides detailed information on the natural history and taxonomy of every invertebrate group of interest to marine aquarists. A superb compilation of vital information and beautiful photos, this book is also an excellent identification guide.
Hard cover, 5½ × 8½", 736 pages
Over 600 full-color photos, many line drawings.